MOUSE ON A STRING

AT THE

PRISON FOR WOMEN

George Caron
(Courtesy Corrections Service Canada Museum)

MOUSE ON A STRING

AT THE

PRISON FOR WOMEN

GEORGE CARON

GENERAL STORE PUBLISHING HOUSE
499 O'Brien Road, Box 415
Renfrew, Ontario, Canada K7V 4A6
Telephone (613) 432-7697 or 1-800-465-6072
www.gsph.com

ISBN 978-1-897508-33-6

Illustration of mouse: Dina Caron
Design and layout: Magdalene Carson / New Leaf Publication Design
Printed by Custom Printers of Renfrew Ltd., Renfrew, Ontario
Printed and bound in Canada

Library and Archives Canada Cataloguing in Publication

Caron, George, 1943-
    Mouse on a string at the Prison for Women / George Caron.
ISBN 978-1-897508-33-6
    1. Prison for Women (Kingston, Ont.). 2. Women prisoners--Ontario--
Kingston. I. Title.
HV9508.K56C35 2009   365'.430971   C2008-908093-9

For Frank W. Anderson, who greatly influenced me and encouraged me to enter adult corrections.

CONTENTS

Prologue / 11

1

Introduction / 15
Protective Custody and Segregation / 27
The Queen Bee / 37
Private Family Visitation (PFV) / 43
The Baseball Team / 45

2

Mary Ann's First Week in the Prison for Women / 48
Mary Ann's Background Offence / 50
Attempted Escape / 58
Mary Ann's Second Christmas / 62
Inappropriate Relationships / 62
The Doukhobors / 65
New Inmates and a Business Proposal / 66
Segregation Visits / 71
Christmas at the P4W / 72
Group Therapy in Protective Custody / 73
Irene's Story / 75

3

The Doukhobors—An Unhealthy Situation / 80
Hostile Acts towards Staff / 82
Inmate Tutoring / 92
Doukhobors' Fasting; Intervention / 92
Prison Entertainment / 99
Frank's Story / 101
Death of Inmate in Segregation / 108

4

Ginger's Nightmare / 111
Pamala's Ordeal / 114
School and Post-Secondary Education / 116
Programs: Mother/Child; Aviary / 118
The Semiahmoo Six Group / 122
Mentally Ill Inmates / 124
Mary Jo's Story / 126

5

Mary's Story / 131
Mouse Meets Jamie / 135
Hiking Adventure / 140
Native Inmates / 142
Mary Ann's Move to the Population / 145

6

The Video Program / 148
The Braille Program / 150
Mary Ann's National Parole Board Experience / 151
Transsexual Inmates (Gender Dysphoria) / 154
Inmates That "Didn't Belong" / 156
Necole's Story / 158
Mary Ann's First Temporary Absence / 159
Male Guards / 161
Mother and Daughter Inmates / 163
Accreditation / 165

7

Mary Ann's Final Days at the Prison for Women / 167
Linda, the Wheeler-Dealer / 168
Inmate Committee Chairpersons / 171
Mary Ann's Release on Full Day Parole / 177
Bomb Threat / 181

8

Mary Ann's College Experiences / 185
Jennifer's Story / 187
Mary Ann's 1986 Christmas / 192
Microfilm Program / 194
More about Mouse / 196

9

Health Care at the PFW / 198
Mary Ann and Brian / 199
Changes to Female Prisons / 201
Isabel McNeill House (IMH) / 202
Female Guards / 204
Mary Ann's Return to the Prison for Women / 207
Mary Ann's Final Release / 211

References / 215
Definitions / 217
Abbreviations and Acronyms / 219
About the Author / 221

PROLOGUE

The Prison For Women, in Kingston, Ontario, operated as Canada's only female maximum security prison from 1934 to 2000. During the span of sixty-four years, many inmates and staff have had a journey through the prison and experienced a new reality that touched their lives and shaped their futures. Some inmates and staff members spent a relatively short period at the prison, while others had to endure many long years. The memories are not all painful. There were times when inmates and staff laughed together and cherished positive experiences.

Over the six decades, there have been many interesting characters who served time at the institution. A few inmates had high profiles that were ceremoniously bestowed on them by various forms of the media, including print (newspapers and books), radio, television, and motion pictures. High-profile inmates like Evelyn Dick, Marlene Moore, and Carla Homolka captured the interest of many Canadians.

From time to time, the makeup of the inmate population would change, attracting new and different segments that influenced how the prison functioned. For example, during the Second World War, some German female aliens were housed at the institution. The 1950s population included females incarcerated for abortion. During the sixties and early seventies, inmates with serious heroin addictions, mostly from Western Canada, found themselves at the prison after convictions for drug-related offences. During the 1960s to the early 1980s, Doukhobor inmates were transferred to the prison. In the eighties, inmates convicted of offences against small children were admitted, and their numbers increased.

It is a sad reality that over the past thirty years, a significant percentage of the population have had Aboriginal backgrounds. Finally, during the last two decades of the prison's existence, the population profile included younger and younger inmates, many convicted of serious violent crimes. The number of inmates serving long sentences and life sentences for murder continued to grow.

I worked at the Prison for Women during the seventies and eighties. My memory bank is filled with the encounters with numerous inmates and staff who influenced my world. Staff at times have a difficult job to do. There is considerable stress that can affect their performance. Equally, inmates have no place to hide and conceal their inner pain. At times I can't stop thinking and reminiscing about the inmates and staff that I had the privilege to supervise and work with at the prison. I am indebted to all the staff and inmates that entered my life.

The different stories and vignettes that I have written about were prompted by actual occurrences. At times I have liberally dramatized the events; it was difficult to stop my imagination from spilling over reality. Sometimes the brutal facts of incarceration revealed the pus and poison that oozes from the unfolding of events and tragic circumstances. I apologize for sometimes portraying events later than they actually occurred or earlier than they were reported.

I have deliberately changed the names of the inmates and staff that were present during my years at the Prison for Women, for obvious reasons. In some instances, I did not change the location where selected inmates were arrested or committed their crime; consequently, it would not be difficult for some inmates to identify themselves. I attempted to be as accurate as possible in reporting the actual events.

I am thankful for the interactions that I experienced with inmates and staff alike. Sometimes, as warden, I had to make difficult decisions that may have been perceived as being too direct and personal. I hold no bad feelings toward any inmates or staff. There were some inmates whom I could not reach or communicate with. In all cases, deep down, I wanted inmates to be successful and live meaningful lives when they returned to the community, without too much hurt or pain from unhappy times. Unfortunately, the inner pain that some inmates had experienced was too great and followed them throughout their lives. I wish there could have been more positive outcomes for the inmates that served time at the prison. I would have liked to see them improved and transformed. It is so rewarding when an inmate changes her life, contributes to the community, and fulfills her goals with happy conclusions.

It is extremely gratifying to acknowledge the gifted people that helped me complete this story. I want to express my thanks to Mary Smith for reviewing my entire manuscript and offering suggestions to improve the document. I would also like to thank Hilton Murray and Sharon Mitchell for their insightful comments on reading portions of the first few chapters of the book. I am especially grateful to my friend Mrs. Marg Ruttan, who was Chief of Health Care during my tenure as warden. Mrs. Ruttan's helpful comments and knowledge about the personalities in the prison helped to shape the framework for this book. Her contribution was most significant and beneficial to me in telling the stories that fill the pages of this book.

I am indebted to David St. Once, the curator of the Correctional Services of Canada's Museum at Kingston, Ontario, for his assistance in obtaining archival material on the Prison for Women.

I would be remiss if I failed to acknowledge Sara Lyman for her intelligent editing skills and suggestions for improving the manuscript. And thanks to Frank Anderson, who had been aware of my plan to write this book for many years; his inspiration helped me to complete this task.

I was fortunate to have three gifted mentors and supervisors during my years in adult corrections who helped to increase my knowledge and understanding of the complex lives of parolees, inmates, and staff experiencing adult penology. My predecessor and former warden; my first supervisor, Mr. Robert Gillies, former District Director of the Edmonton Parole Office; and Mr. Arthur Trono, Deputy Commissioner of the Ontario Region Correctional Service of Canada. These gentlemen were truly good role models and an inspiration to me.

During the 1980s while I was warden, the Correctional Service of Canada was headed by Mr. Donald Yeomans. In my opinion, he was probably one of the most influential commissioners that CSC ever had. He helped to advance program opportunities for inmates in prisons and in the community and to provide opportunities for staff to raise CSC's image in Canada and the world.

Producing a manuscript is only the first part of the experience. Getting the manuscript published is the real challenge. Rejection letters are difficult to accept, but they help to reaffirm one's determination to proceed with the struggle. I appreciated the encouragement and enthusiastic support of two new local writers, Peter Hennessy and Nancy Brown. Their support and belief in this project, as well as sharing their knowledge of how the book publishing business operates, were greatly appreciated.

I would like to thank Mr. Tim Gordon of General Store Publishing House, who saw the merits of my manuscript and is prepared to publish it. I would like to express my gratitude to Senior Editor Jane Karchmar for the final editing and constructive criticism to improve the final product.

Last, I would like to express my sincere appreciation to my wife, Dina, and my children, Necole, Elisabeth, and Michael, who had to serve as sounding boards when progress on the manuscript was going slowly and problems were in abundance. I thank my family for allowing me the opportunity to escape briefly into my office to write and research this book.

1

Introduction

It was early morning when I boarded a 727 jet heading west to Vancouver from Toronto. I was tired after staying up the night before trying to convince a young Native woman to hand over the small razor blade that she was using to carve up her arms.

Her blood had flowed like lava. Her low cries for help were deeply embedded in my mind. I was depressed when I thought of the endless battles trying to reach Emma. The staff did everything they could to save her, including bringing in an Elder leader from up north. I recalled her last words: "Warden! Help my sisters." There is nothing more disheartening than the death of an inmate in segregation. Prisons are unhealthy environments that can occasionally erupt like volcanoes.

As a male from Western Canada with a Native background, I am saddened that so many Aboriginal women come from communities across Canada where poverty, inadequate housing, lack of educational opportunities, unemployment, poor health, excessive alcoholism, and drugs exist.

I was happy that no one sat beside me during the first segment of the flight. I was upset and needed to recharge my batteries. Emma's whispers were penetrating my psyche. I was going home. I needed a little time to be with my family while I toured several female prisons in Washington State and British Columbia.

Shortly after the plane drifted over the Rockies, I watched a young, attractive woman slither down the aisle, heading toward me. She had penetrating dark eyes that captured my interest. Her perfume opened my veins and infused new life into my soul.

"Good morning! Do you mind if I sit beside you? There is a small kid up there that will not stop crying."

I responded, "No problem. I will move my papers."

A few minutes passed as she gazed out of the window to observe the white, misty clouds and then glanced at the notes that were over my knees. I was surprised when she opened up. "My name is Joy. I am heading to Vancouver to give a paper at Simon Fraser University, where the Western Biological and Wildlife Society is conducting their annual meeting. I've just finished working five long months up north, studying polar bears."

She seemed to want human conversation, but abruptly stopped herself and cocooned her thoughts. I sensed that she wanted to talk but did not want to appear to be too friendly. A few minutes passed, and I responded. "My name is George; I am going to the West Coast to visit my family and complete a little business." Joy seemed to be a little bit pompous, having little time for the simple, mundane things of life. Perhaps the isolation may have affected her social abilities. Joy stated that she was a scientist with a mission to reveal to the world the mating habits of Arctic polar bears.

"What takes you to Vancouver? Are you a businessman?" She turned her head a little and concentrated on looking outside the window at the distant snow-covered peaks, as well as sizing up my dark hair and silver-framed glasses. Joy seemed genuinely interested in my background.

Apprehensively, I responded, "I'm the warden of a female maximum security prison and I am taking some time to visit several female prisons."

With a look of amazement, Joy asked, "You really are the warden of a female prison?"

After a long pause, I replied, "Yes. It's a difficult job at times, but I enjoy my work."

Joy's face tensed up and she remarked in a negative manner, "I would not want your job. How could you work with those dangerous, men-hating women? But I imagine it is like working in a sewer; in time you become acclimatized."

I retrenched and could see that nothing would interest her unless it involved biology and the mating habits of polar bears. I turned my head sharply and took solace from the events outside. It was raining heavily as we got closer to Vancouver. The rain pounded on the windows. A few minutes later, there was an announcement from the flight crew: "Good afternoon; this is the captain. Within twenty minutes, we will be landing in beautiful Vancouver. It is seventy-two degrees and raining. I hope you brought your umbrella. The staff and I wish you a good day, and we thank you for flying Air Canada."

It was almost four p.m. when I gathered my bags and headed for a friendly smile at a nearby car rental. The passengers dispersed into the parking lot and adjacent roadway, searching for transportation to take them into the belly of the city. Vancouver was indeed a beautiful city. Travelling over a large bridge, I looked up and could see the white-draped mountains stretching down to the blue inlet of open water, where numerous small and large boats lay at anchor in the bay. The city was alive with motion and activity everywhere—rush hour, a human anthill. In a little over one hour, I would be in my parents' home. As I stopped at a red light, my thoughts centred on my youth in Vancouver and momentarily I drifted off. Suddenly, an irate taxicab driver honked his horn. "Get going! Welcome to rush hour traffic!"

It was difficult to drive in the old neighbourhood without being swallowed up by emotion. My past life flashed by as I passed near my former high school. I remembered the football and basketball games that pushed fall and winter days into moments of ecstasy. I could feel the ghosts and spirits of past years standing guard at the entrance to my old high school. Of course, we were good and proud of our team. The years had gone and taken their toll. Few of my teammates remained in the neighbourhood.

A few minutes passed as I circled the town's graveyard. I couldn't go by without stopping and paying my respects to Ann Marie, the best cheerleader at our school when I was in my teens. Ann Marie died prematurely one cold winter night after being hit by a drunk driver. Her tombstone pushes my mind into fast reverse. Why her? Why my old girlfriend? I still get upset at this senseless crime.

A short distance away, I entered the street where my parents' house was located. My parents still lived in the same house where I grew up. It was good to see my mother's and father's faces when I opened the basement door and started to climb up the narrow stairs to the kitchen. Mother was in her early sixties and had traces of grey. She was a kind woman who cared deeply. Dad was close to seventy and still full of energy. He carried his years well. He had dark hair with strong features. His picture on the kitchen mantel could have passed for the Godfather.

As I entered the kitchen, I observed Mom toiling as usual at the stove, preparing dinner for the family. She was serving a life sentence. My parents were honest, hard-working people, strong, practising Roman Catholics. I had been gifted with two strong anchors in my corner. Mom gave me a big kiss and hug. "How is my number one son?" Sometimes it is difficult being the oldest of seven children! Dad and I hugged and held onto each other for a few minutes. It is different when two males hug and hold each other; it is a more secure feeling than hugging my mom.

Dad said, "We thought that you would be coming in tomorrow. It's nice to have you home early."

I replied, "I received a call a few days ago from the airline representative stating that my original flight had a cancellation and that if I wanted I could take advantage of flying home on Friday instead of Saturday. How is retirement, Dad?"

"Great! Terry [my youngest brother] and I go fishing for salmon every week; they are truly gifts from the mighty Fraser River." Dad grabbed my bags and placed them in my old bedroom.

"Wow! Where is Terry?"

Mom responded, "Where else? He is down at Boston Bar with Keno [his large German shepherd] trying to bring home a big fish for supper."

Terry was twenty-one and the last-born. He was a big kid who never really wanted to grow up. He loved his life the way things were: fishing, fishing, and drinking. I was concerned about him. Living in the East for so long, I found it difficult—almost impossible—to influence his ways.

Terry reminded me of Leonard, the old bachelor alcoholic who had lived next door for years with his mother. He did everything for his mother until the first of the month, when her cheque disappeared into drink. It was sad, but I saw Terry travelling on the same train. He was good for my parents but so dependent on them. Terry was a trucker, but had a difficult time finding a job.

It was almost six p.m. Dad said, "Turn on the radio." He was addicted to news programs. He loved his TV, radio, and newspaper. My dad had a long love affair with the radio. I can remember as a boy sharing the corner of the living room as we huddled like scrum backfielders over a ball. In addition, we enjoyed the old radio programs such as Friday night boxing, *The Shadow*, *Gunsmoke*, *Amos and Andy*, *Gangbusters*, etc. There was something magical about radio. You could use your imagination to dress a scene in a story.

"Looks like another strike," Dad remarked.

I responded, "Who is striking now, Dad?"

"International Woodworkers of America and the paper mills at the same time. We will shut them down." My dad was a strong union man, married to the New Democratic Party.

After sitting down and saying grace, Mom asked, "Do you want one or two pork chops?"

"I am not that hungry; I will only have one, thank you."

It was almost six forty-five p.m. when we finished supper. I explained to my parents that I would be home for a few days only. On Monday, I would be visiting a women's prison in Burnaby, and on Tuesday morning I would be travelling to Gig Harbor, Washington, to visit another female prison. "George, do you want some dessert, love?" My mother always had dessert. She always baked cookies and other goodies. With a large family, Mom knew how to satisfy our wants.

While we were enjoying a coffee, I heard Keno barking outside. "Could that be the fishing team? Any luck?" I yelled down to the basement.

Terry replied, "Sadly, no, they weren't biting." Terry put his fishing gear away and joined us. "Hi, brother," he greeted me, giving me a high five. "How are you? How is the family?"

"Dina and the kids are fine. I am home for a few days. How is Keno?" The dog was married to Terry. Wherever Terry was, so was his dog, Keno.

"His hips are bothering him; it looks like he will experience the same problem his father had."

Later that night, Dad, Terry, and I watched the playoff hockey game. Mom as usual grabbed her book and headed to bed early.

After dinner on Saturday, I telephoned one of my high school friends and one of my sisters who lived close to my mom and dad. I also telephoned a former professor and my first-year field supervisor of my Masters of Social Work degree, who was visiting Vancouver to participate in an international corrections conference. Frank was a unique individual who was instrumental in getting me and a female classmate into Federal Corrections. Frank encouraged me to apply for a Solicitor General's Scholarship, which I did, successfully. Both Pat and I were initially interested in other areas, but with Frank's positive encouragement and his firm direction and determination, he led his two students into the world of adult penology.

Now, as I talked to Frank on the phone, he opened up and shared a little bit of his life. He revealed that he had served a life sentence in Saskatchewan Penitentiary. I was totally blown away on hearing Frank's words! He thought it was time to tell me a little of his background. Frank stated he was going to give a lecture at the conference on prison reform. He expressed his happiness in having recruited Pat and me to work in corrections. I responded that I believed Frank's story was compelling and needed to be told. After this eventful call, I was tired. I said goodnight to my parents and Terry and fell into bed.

On Monday morning, I jumped into the rental car and headed for Oakalla Prison, located about twenty miles away in Burnaby near Vancouver. Oakalla Prison was a very old provincial fenced prison that housed both male and female inmates, in two separate facilities. I had entered Oakalla Prison previously (approximately twenty years before) when I visited a cousin who was incarcerated for eighteen months on a theft charge. I was nineteen years old at the time, and I was put through the wringer as guards searched my clothing and body for contraband.

It haunted me to enter the prison again. This time my admission was uneventful. After providing my identification papers, I was allowed into the prison grounds. The female warden had left a note at the front entrance that provided details of my visit.

After signing in the admission book, the guard in charge of the front entry station directed me to the female enclosure. "Keep to the right—you can't miss it." Like the large male prison, the buildings housing the female inmates were also old. The female prison was surrounded by a twelve-foot metal fence. At the time of my visit (1980), there were ninety-three inmates incarcerated there, serving sentences of up to two years less one day. There were also inmates awaiting sentencing, and, in addition, there were three federal inmates awaiting transfer to the Prison for Women in Kingston, Ontario.

When I entered the female unit, I was escorted to the warden's office. I waited for ten minutes, because the female warden was busy managing a small crisis. At 8:45 a.m., the warden, Mary, entered the visiting room and invited me into her office. She was an experienced, tough-talking woman who had been working at Oakalla for twenty years. Mary was an attractive woman in her late forties. She was neatly dressed and had her long, dark hair done up in a bun. She had a lazy eye that continued to blink incessantly; she got my attention.

I received the impression that Mary was a no-nonsense manager who ensured that her staff followed the prison's rules and regulations. She explained to me that two inmates had tried to escape from the prison last week and were caught trying to scale the fence behind the main cellblock. She pointed to the blind spot that needed to be corrected.

Mary asked how long I had been at the Prison for Women. I said about five years. She laughed and said that I was very young to be a warden. I commented that at age thirty-six, I was the youngest warden in Federal Corrections at that time.

Mary appeared to be a little apprehensive of my youth, but, before I left her institution three hours later, she commented that although I was young, the mentoring I had received from the previous male warden at the Prison for Women had surely helped me to effectively deal with the varied and complex issues facing a warden. Mary explained that she had spoken to Murray White several times during the past three years, and he said that he was leaving his post because of health issues, but thought that I was ready to assume the leadership role. It was funny, but I never fully realized that Murray had all along been helping me to better understand the warden's role and the complexities of Canada's only female maximum security prison.

After visiting two living units and several work areas, Mary invited me to lunch. I remember the lunch: beans and wieners. The beans were overcooked and the wieners shrivelled up like small, dried dates. I thought to myself that the PFW made better meals. During the lunch, Mary and I talked about inmates who had spent time at Oakalla and eventually were incarcerated at Prison for Women.

Mary asked how Norma[1] was making out. Norma was a twenty-nine-year-old white female who had escaped twelve times from several provincial lockup facilities in British Columbia before she escaped again from Oakalla. Each time, she was out for only a few weeks before she was caught. I remarked that when Norma was transferred to the Prison for Women, I interviewed her, and she commented, "I will escape from your prison before I am thirty." Nine months had passed at that point since her arrival. I'd had her watched daily the first six months to make sure her prediction was not realized. The previous two months, I'd had her staying in segregation because she tried to stab another inmate during a fight.

After lunch, Mary escorted me to the school area. I talked to several inmate students and observed their surroundings. The school was small and old. It did not appear to provide the appropriate atmosphere for learning. One young female teacher was charged with providing instruction to eleven students. I noticed one inmate locked in another part of the library. Mary said that was Mary Ann. At first, I was not particularly interested in talking to this woman, but Mary mentioned that Mary Ann was serving a life sentence and was to be transferred to the Prison for Women when her appeal was completed in four weeks.

A correctional officer opened the locked door, and Mary and I entered. Mary Ann was a shy young woman who did not speak freely. Shortly after we entered the room, the warden was called away to resolve a matter. I introduced myself and informed Mary Ann I worked in corrections. I sat down on the other side of the

---

1   I have changed all names.

table. Mary Ann was a twenty-three-year-old white American woman sentenced for kidnapping a baby from a large hospital in the Vancouver area. Mary Ann had sandy-coloured hair and beautiful blue eyes. She was a plain Jane; no makeup, no perfume, and wore simple prison clothes. She was about five feet, seven inches tall. She had a slim build and a nice figure, but desperately needed a major make-over.

Her head was bent low and she seldom looked up when she spoke. She had a strong body odour and could have used a bath or shower. Mary Ann mentioned that she had a Grade 7 education but that she could not read or write very well. When I told her that I was the warden at the Prison for Women, she opened up a little bit, and some sunshine captured her facial expression. She said in a low voice, "Can't speak." I said it was okay. Although I had interviewed many hundreds of inmates, something attracted me to Mary Ann's situation.

Mary Ann was brewing coffee and asked if I wanted a cup. I said I would be pleased to have a coffee. She turned around and bent down to pour the coffee into two mugs, her shirt riding up a bit. When Mary Ann was turned completely away, I observed a large tattoo on her lower back near her buttocks. It was a coloured image of a mouse on a string. This image entered my psyche. It was a beautiful tattoo of a mouse with large eyes, one blue and one brown. I was completely surprised to view the tattoo, but made no reference to it. The image of the mouse has remained in my memory to this day.

I encouraged Mary Ann to take high school courses and read with a dictionary by her side. I told her that there was a large school area at the Prison for Women and that education was the key to opening doors for her. A few minutes later, the warden appeared and said that we should continue with our tour. I said good bye to Mary Ann, informing her that it was a pleasure to have met her, and that I looked forward to her arriving at the Prison for Women.

After the warden and I left the school area, Mary indicated that Mary Ann was in protected custody because of her offence, and that she had had a rough time when she was first admitted to the institution. In prison, female inmates—like male inmates—have no use for inmates who commit offences against children. Looking back, I suspect that Mary Ann's low self-image might have been a way to avoid contact with other people who had possibly found out about her offence and the reason for her being in prison.

The next building the warden took me to was the institutional kitchen. It was a beehive of activity. Many of the new inmates worked in the kitchen. Looking out the kitchen window, I noticed a small building a little bigger than a house that was completely covered in tin and metal. I asked the warden what was in that building. Mary said we were going there next and it would be an eye-opener for me.

The warden obtained a key and arranged for a guard to be posted outside the main entrance. We walked inside the metal building, and, once inside, I observed two middle-aged women (late fifties or sixties) inside the unit. The warden told me that the two women were ringleaders of the Sons of Freedom Doukhobor Sect.

The Doukhobors were members of a 200-year-old Christian sect originally from Russia that traditionally believed that every person knew what was right and must be guided by this knowledge rather than by any outside authority or government. In 1898, several thousand Doukhobors left Russia and settled mainly in Western Canada.[2] The original group of Doukhobors split into three groups. The largest sector was the Orthodox (community) group. The next largest group was the Sons of Freedom Sect. The smallest group was the Independent. Most of the Orthodox and Independent Doukhobors broke out of the tight, inbred world in which the Sons of Freedom Sect existed. The name "Doukhobor" (Russian *doukhobortsi*, spirit-wrestlers) was given to them by the Russian Orthodox Church, which claimed that they were wrestling against the Holy Spirit.[3]

The Sons of Freedom Doukhobor Sect was the most radical group of Doukhobors. Members frequently burned property

2   *Canadian Intermediate Dictionary* (Toronto: Gage Publishing Ltd., 1979), 348.
3   Simma Holt, *Terror in the Name of God* (Toronto: McClelland and Stewart Limited, 1964), 10.

of the other rival Doukhobor groups. They burned many government buildings (causing millions of dollars in damages) and rail-
road installations. After fires were set, the Doukhobor clan would
strip naked. They believed that clothing had become a device to
conceal that which was called "shame."[4]

Both women had been incarcerated for arson: burning down
a school and a government building. The warden introduced me
to them. She told them, "Mr. Caron is the warden of the Prison
for Women at Kingston, Ontario." The warden stated that Marta
B. and Molly A. were being transferred to the Prison for Women
in three weeks. Both women were serving eight- and nine-year
sentences.

It was strange, but the two female inmates never said a word.
They looked at me with great distaste. The hatred oozed out of
their bodies. They had devil images about their beings. I noticed
on a small table, bread, salt, and a dish of water. I did not realize it
then, but these items were the Doukhobors' symbol of life.

As we turned away to walk out of the building, I smelled a
strange odour. We turned around and noticed that the two women
had taken off all their clothing and were completely naked. They
had retrieved matches from their body cavities or sweaters and
started fires in two metal garbage cans. The dark smoke filled
the air. I thought to myself, *the devil is here*. The breasts of the
two older inmates hung low almost to their navels. The older of
the two female inmates (Marta) yelled, "Warden, make room for
us. We are coming to your prison, and will present problems for
you and your staff. We will burn your facility down." They then
briefly spoke Doukhobor (one of the Russian dialects) in a slow
chant, bowing their heads and raising their hands above their
heads. The warden called for staff to enter the building and put
clothes on the two inmates.

I mentioned to Mary that we had seven Doukhobor inmates
at the Prison for Women, and that we were keeping a close watch
on them to ensure that they did not start fires. I must admit — the
two Doukhobor inmate leaders created a foreboding introduction.

---

4   Ibid., 102.

I really did not know how much they would impact me during the next few years.

The next morning, I got up early with the birds and headed south into Washington State. I was travelling to Gig Harbor, a small community south of Tacoma, Washington, about four hours from Vancouver, British Columbia. I had made arrangements to tour the Purdy Treatment Centre for Women.[5] On the way, I passed Bellingham, Washington, home of Western Washington State College,[6] my former undergraduate college in the late sixties. Memories crowded my thoughts as I drove by the sign exiting to the university. I'd had some good years at Western Washington State University.

When I arrived at the Purdy institution, I was surprised to see a modern facility with a high metal fence around the perimeter. The institution looked more like a junior college campus than a state institution for female offenders.

The warden had arranged a comprehensive tour. I was truly impressed with the facilities. I was especially interested in the staff arrangement, including a well-educated young man and woman. The Purdy had 210 inmates inside its fence. In addition, I was really impressed with a large halfway facility outside the fence where the majority of the inmates resided at one time or another on their way back into the community. The warden indicated that there were two Canadian inmates at Purdy. One inmate was serving twelve years for bank robbery in Seattle. While touring a vocational shop, I heard an inmate call my name. I turned around and noticed a cleaner in one of the rooms. "How are you, Mr. Caron?"

I was surprised to see April, a thirty-four-year-old black woman, at the Purdy. April was a hard-core drug addict who had done time for drugs at the Prison for Women. She was serving ten years for conveying narcotics into Washington State.

April said, "I much preferred the Prison for Women instead of Purdy."

---

5   In 1996, its name was changed to the Washington Corrections Centre for Women.

6   In the U.S. in those days, a college was equivalent to a university; their junior college was equivalent to the Canadian college; the term "college" has now, with some exceptions, been replaced by "university."

I asked why, and she commented, "At the Prison for Women, staff openly allowed inmates to have relationships with other inmates. It is not the same at the Purdy."

I wished April good luck with her future. It was sad, but I suspected April would return to the Prison for Women in the future, since she was heavily involved in the use and selling of hard drugs in Canada.

After I returned to my parents' home much later the same day, I was advised that I had received a telephone call from Mary, the warden at Oakalla Prison. She reported that Mary Ann (of the mouse tattoo) had enjoyed our conversation and looked forward to improving her education at Prison for Women.

The next morning, I caught the early flight to Toronto. I'd had a good visit with my family and benefitted from the tour of both Oakalla Prison and the Purdy Treatment Centre for Women. I was tired and had no problem catching a little sleep.

I woke up about one and a half hours later. I looked out the window, and my mind kept returning to the three new people that had entered my life in the past two days. I was totally surprised by Frank's admission that he had served a life sentence. I wanted to know much more, but I had not felt it was appropriate to question him during our short phone call. In future years, Frank's life would intersect with mine and compel me to tell his story. Equally compelling, my working life at the Prison for Women was caught up in the story of Mary Ann and the two Doukhobor women.

Protective Custody and Segregation

The Prison for Women was Canada's only maximum-security female prison. It was a walled institution within an eight-acre parcel of land located near Kingston Penitentiary and Lake Ontario. Inmates serving sentences of two years or more came from all provinces and territories. In addition, there were two juvenile inmates under nineteen years of age, who were transferred to the Prison for Women under the federal/provincial exchange agreements. These young inmates were transferred to the PFW because provincial jail staff could either not manage these tough, difficult inmates or they did not have the appropriate facilities to manage an inmate with a long sentence.

We had, at that time, 121 inmates serving a variety of offences, including murder, manslaughter, aggravated assault, robbery, kidnapping, drug trafficking, and so on. The average sentence was three years, ten months. There were thirty-six inmates serving life or long sentences for murder or manslaughter. There were ten foreign inmates at the prison serving sentences mainly for drug trafficking. The majority of these inmates were well educated, but due to circumstances had agreed to be "mules," carrying drugs on their bodies or in their bags as they entered Canada from various South American or Asian countries. Once caught and tried by a court, they would receive a minimum sentence of seven years.

Prison for Women entrance, 1965; you can see my office to the left of the door, on the first floor (indicated by the arrows). My secretary's office is to the extreme left.
(Courtesy Corrections Service Canada Museum)

Aerial view of Prison for Women, Kingston Penitentiary, and Queen's University Faculty of Education McArthur Hall.
(Courtesy Corrections Service Canada Museum)

There are many stories around the Prison for Women. I will concentrate on Mary Ann's life as well as that of some of the other inmates and try to make sense of their time at the PFW and their impact on me as a young warden of a female maximum security prison. I met many interesting people while working as a warden in corrections. For a lot of personal reasons, Mary Ann's story in particular needs to be told.

I arrived back in Kingston late Wednesday night. I was exhausted, but happy to spend a few precious hours with my wife and family. My wife asked, "How was your trip?"

I commented that it was interesting, to say the least. "While I toured both Oakalla and the Purdy institution, I met an interesting young American inmate serving a life sentence for kidnapping a baby, and two middle-aged female leaders of the Doukhobor sect. In addition, I had a good telephone conversation with Frank Anderson."

"Who is Frank Anderson?"

"Remember Mr. Anderson? He was my field supervisor during my first-year placement in the Masters of Social Work program. Frank told me that he had served a life sentence and was imprisoned in Saskatchewan Penitentiary."

My wife changed the subject. "How is your family?"

"Fine. Terry is drinking too much, Dad is enjoying his retirement, and Mom continues to look after the house and family."

The next morning, I arrived early at the Prison for Women. I received a full briefing from the Assistant Warden Security (AW Security). She said, "There were some problems with the seven Doukhobor inmates. I am glad you are back." The assistant warden was an experienced, middle-aged woman with motherly instincts. She wore her uniform proudly and would pass any military inspection. She was always dressed properly. She had raised eleven children. Mary could be compassionate and fair and equally tough-minded if required.

She reported that one of the Doukhobor inmates had started a small cell fire and that it could have gotten much worse. The staff rushed to the cell as smoke billowed out onto the range landing. Mary reported that one older (late forties), heavy-set matron named Jenny grabbed a fire extinguisher and tried to put out the small fire. A Doukhobor inmate was naked and stood in front of the cell chanting a ritual prayer.

The guard, in some distress, yelled, "The fire extinguisher isn't working. Bring me another damned extinguisher!" A second guard standing close by rushed over to the cell with a second fire extinguisher. She emptied its contents, spreading it all over the fire and the cell. The assistant warden explained that two other small cell fires had occurred the same day, so they placed all seven Doukhobor inmates in segregation. Somehow the Doukhobor inmates in the prison appeared to be aware that their two ringleaders would soon be arriving at the prison.

Mary explained that all the Doukhobor inmates in segregation were naked and refused to wear the pyjamas issued to them.

She looked at me and asked, "How was your trip?"

I said, "It went okay. Incidentally, I met Marta B. and Molly A., the two leaders of the Doukhobor Sons of Freedom Sect in

British Columbia. They indicated that we could expect problems when they arrive later this month.

"Mary, you won't believe me when I tell you what happened in Oakalla Prison. Late in the afternoon, the warden brought me to a small metal building. Inside were Marta B. and Molly A. They had the look of the devil in their eyes. As we were leaving the building, the warden and I smelled something. We turned around and observed that both ladies had taken all their clothes off. They were buck naked. The two inmates had taken matches from their body cavities or sweaters and started fires in two metal waste baskets. Marta B. said in broken English, 'Warden, make room for us. We are coming to your prison and will present problems for you and your staff. We will burn your facility down.'" I looked Mary straight in the eye and said, "It was unreal. It was like the devil was speaking to me. I think we will have problems whey they arrive.

"By the way, I met an American white girl who is serving a life sentence for kidnapping a baby. I suspect she will be arriving at the end of the month. When she arrives, we will have to place her in protective custody."

Mary said that the two French sisters who had been transferred in from Quebec overdosed last night on homemade brew and pills and had been taken by ambulance to Hotel Dieu Hospital. They would survive and would be returned later this afternoon.

Before leaving my office, the assistant warden laughed out loud and said, "There was one more incident last night."

I said, "Give me the goods."

"Well, Officer Soave [an older French-Canadian woman in her early fifties who had a serious drinking problem] did something stupid."

"Please explain."

Mary could no longer hold her laughter. I shouted, "Come on!"

"Well, she must have been a little tipsy—she dropped the large main range [folger lock][7] key in the toilet, and it was flushed down into the main drain."

---

7   The folger key (a very large metal key) opened the major security
    areas in the prison, the hospital, and the narcotics safe. It was a very
    important key and was controlled each shift by security staff.

"My God! Could inmates get access to the large key?"

"No—I directed the plumber to see if he could retrieve it down at the bend in the pipe in the basement, but no luck. He said, 'The key is gone. Looking in the sewer pipe would be a real dirty job.'"

The assistant warden did a good job when I was away, but when there were many balls in the air, she would get agitated and bitchy. Nevertheless, I was glad to have Mary as my Assistant Warden Security. She was a straight shooter and willing to roll up her sleeves and pitch in if things got out of control.

Protective Custody, lower floor.
(Author)

The next day, I toured the prison and spent about one hour meeting with inmates in protective custody (PC) and the segregation unit proper. Inmates placed in protective custody in segregation were there mainly as my guests or because they couldn't live in the general prison population and requested protection.

The protective custody cell block had ten cells in it and was located at the rear of the main building, separated from all living units. It was a locked, secure area. The range had an upper tier and a lower tier, with five cells per tier. One cell on the lower tier was used as an office for the two security officers who supervised the protective custody area and the larger segregation cell range. The two correctional officers had access to a telephone and walkie-talkies. Each cell had a toilet, sink, and metal bunk bed with blanket and sheets. In addition, there was a small dresser in each cell. Inmates could put pictures on the walls. As well, one cell in the lower tier of PC was used for bathing and the storage of linens. Another cell was used as a TV room. Inmates in the PC area were allowed to make coffee and tea on the lower tier landing. Nurses made medical rounds four times per day in segregation to dispense medication and check on the well-being of both the PC inmates and inmates in segregation proper.

At the time, there were ten inmates in segregation. Five inmates were in PC because they had committed offences against children like murder, incest, attempted murder, child sexual abuse, and assault. In addition, there was one inmate up in the second-floor tier for six years. This inmate had given testimony in court against organized crime mob leaders in British Columbia. Her testimony resulted in two male leaders' receiving life sentences for murder. The mob had placed a contract out on her life. The other inmate upstairs was in PC for stabbing an inmate leader in the prison during a fight. She was in PC because she was in danger of being killed if returned to the general population.

The other secure area in segregation consisted of fourteen cells. There were five cells in the lower tier and nine cells in the upper tier. One cell in each of the lower and upper tiers was used for bathing and the storage of linens. At the time of my visit, there were seven Doukhobor inmates in segregation and three other inmates for disciplinary reasons. The majority of inmates were placed in segregation because of serious behavioural problems or because they had been convicted in disciplinary court.

Inmates in PC were allowed radios and program materials in their cells. The inmates in this section were generally not locked up in their cells during the day and early evening. When staff or visitors entered the segregation area and passed through the PC area to the segregation side, the PC inmates were locked up in their cells before the entrance door was opened. Inmates in protective custody were allowed to keep cigarettes and matches in their cells.

Inmates in the disciplinary area of segregation were all dressed in prison pyjamas. Each cell contained a toilet, sink, and metal bunk bed with blanket and sheets. The cell bars were all painted black to better assist correctional officers in viewing inmates inside their cells. Inmates were allowed showers or baths two to three times per week. Sheets of toilet paper were handed out by the staff as they were needed. This method helped prevent upset inmates from blocking their toilets with rolls of toilet paper or starting fires. There were no visitors allowed in segregation. PC inmates who received visitors were placed in a closed, separate, monitored cell in the visiting and correspondence area one afternoon per week or when special arrangements were made.

All inmates in segregation, whether in the PC area or general segregation area, were high up in the building (second floor) and could look out of their cells through the bars and have a direct view of the Queen's University teacher's college located across the street from the prison's eighteen-foot perimeter wall. One radio was allowed to be on in the segregation area. During the summer months, inmates in segregation were allowed to go down the back stairs each day and exercise for an hour in a secure area away from the general prison population. During the winter months, inmates were allowed thirty minutes of daily exercise. Inmates in segregation could write letters if they acted responsibly, and they were allowed one cigarette per hour. The guards (matrons) were frequently passing out cigarettes each hour and lighting them. Doukhobor inmates were not allowed matches, paper, or cigarettes.

The inmates in PC status required a lot of attention. I routinely went from cell to cell and inquired how each inmate was doing. The majority of these inmates required a lot of time. They asked questions about their individual cases and inquired about programs for the group. Sometimes an inmate would ask how her former girlfriend was doing and what was happening in the population.

I entered the locked segregation unit. The female guard yelled, "Man on the range! Please be decent." I inspected the two tiers of the range. I observed that two uniformed members of the Salvation Army were just leaving the segregation range. The

Segregation cells.
(Author)

Salvation Army volunteers visited the segregation unit once per week. The two female officers said hello as they signed out and exited the range. I have a lot of respect for the Salvation Army and the work they do in and out of prison. On a number of occasions, the Salvation Army members would ask to see me to discuss issues related to selected inmates. Most of the inmates placed in segregation because of extreme behavioural problems were not interested in talking unless they were not getting their cigarettes, baths, or exercise periods.

All the Doukhobor inmates in segregation were naked. They refused to put their clothes on unless one of the guards opened a window to let in some fresh air or remove the smoke that filled the air.

They were all in their mid-forties or older. The majority of them were overweight and not very attractive. I spent a short time with each of them. They did not try to cover their bodies. In fact, they seemed to take pleasure in trying to embarrass me. I must admit that the bodies of the Doukhobor inmates did not affect my emotions. They had one thing in common: they did not appear to have used breast support prior to coming to prison. Furthermore, most of the women had unshaved legs. I left the area with no requests for food, programs, or visits.

The next day, I was in my office when my secretary knocked on my door. She was a thin lady in her late forties or early fifties. She had worked as a secretary for the previous two wardens. She said, "The Inmate Sentence Administrator would like to see you."

I said, "Have her come in."

The Inmate Sentence Administrator was a very small, high-energy woman in her late forties. She had the habit of speaking quickly. She entered my office and advised me that she had received information that four federal inmates, including the two Doukhobor leaders, were coming to the PFW in fourteen days. I asked her to make sure they had all their medical files and papers that stated they were free of infectious disease.

About six months before, this Inmate Sentence Administrator had made a major human error. It was her job to check all new inmates' medical files during the day shift before a new inmate was admitted into the institution. A letter would be on file from the doctor at the sending institution that verified the inmate was free of infectious disease. In this instance, the Inmate Sentence Administrator failed to check the medical release form on a new inmate named Betty, who had just arrived at the institution. Two weeks after she was admitted to the institution, it was determined that Betty had a very active case of infectious tuberculosis and had to be placed in a secure hospital isolation room in a military hospital.

The inmate in question was originally charged with robbery and sentenced to eighteen months in the Vanier Institution for Women near Toronto. She had escaped from the provincial jail and killed a man one night. Betty was captured and sentenced to life for murder. Given her maximum security status, two correctional officers were assigned each shift (three shifts per day) to supervise Betty at the military hospital. Betty remained in the isolation room at the military hospital for five months. The overtime bill was approximately $80,000, plus a hospital bill that was $100,000. This was a very costly mistake. It could have been much worse if staff and inmates at the prison had been infected with tuberculosis.

It was no wonder that every time we received a new inmate, I reminded the Inmate Sentence Administrator to be sure that there was a waiver in the inmate's file stating she was free of infectious disease. I had instructed the Inmate Sentence Administrator that if the waiver was not signed by a doctor, under no circumstances was the inmate to be admitted into the prison.

The Queen Bee

The following year brought many challenging duties. Prior to becoming warden, I had watched with interest how the previous warden interacted with and managed a Queen Bee named Marlene. In all my years at the Prison for Women, I experienced only one Queen Bee. Three years later, I had an opportunity to interview an old correctional officer who had started when the Prison for Women opened in 1934. She told me there had been some aggressive, intelligent, informal inmate leaders over the years, but none had reached the heights or level of being a true Queen Bee.

The Queen Bee (Marlene) was an inmate that ruled the nest. She was the top inmate and received total allegiance and respect from most inmates and even some staff. Her influence was surprising. The Queen Bee had tremendous control over inmates with limited education and understanding. Other inmates with intelligence and some power never took her on.

The Queen Bee was a forty-nine-year-old heavy-set woman with reddish, dirty blonde hair. She had freckles on her face and hands. When upset or mad, her eyes would seem to enlarge and paralyze her adversaries. It was spellbinding. Marlene controlled relationships with both inmates and some staff. Few wanted to cross her. Marlene was a hardened alcoholic with a plethora of psychological problems. She was serving a life sentence for murder. She had killed her first husband by stabbing him during a drunken orgy in 1965. She was charged with murder, but in 1966, her lawyer got her off with a rare and special defence of "automatism."

Basically, the defence centred on extreme alcoholism. It was generally a one-time defence strategy. In 1966, her lawyer, using the testimony of a noted psychiatrist, proved to the judge and jury that she was too drunk to fully appreciate and understand the nature of her actions. The judge ruled that she be acquitted of the murder charge.

Reviewing the law books, I found that automatism was "a term used to describe unconscious involuntary behaviour, the state of a person who though capable of action, is not conscious of what he [or she] is doing. It means an unconscious involuntary act, where the mind does not go with what is being done."[8]

In 1970, Marlene was drinking heavily again. One night she killed her second husband by stabbing him during a drunken rage. The same court judge that presided over Marlene's first murder trial found her guilty and sentenced her to life.

Marlene surrounded herself with criminally minded inmates—those who had the compulsion to steal, cheat, rob, use drugs, or commit any acts to benefit themselves. Marlene had received the sympathy of other inmates because she was the longest-serving lifer in the prison. She milked this reality to the nth degree.

The former warden used Marlene to move his agenda. He allowed her certain things in her cell in exchange for information about activities in the prison. She was not a rat, but helped the warden understand the dynamics of his charges. Sometime she could resolve problems between inmates. Many times, the previous warden would consult with staff, but also with Marlene to get an assurance that a given inmate in segregation would not be in harm's way if returned to the open population.

When I took over full time as acting warden in 1979, my style was different than that of the former warden. I found it difficult to seek information from Marlene, or to receive her blessing on some issues. It was my belief that the prison would be a better environment if no Queen Bee were present. Marlene viewed me as a real threat to her empire. She manipulated things and issues to cause me grief.

---

8   R.V.K. (1971) 3 CCC (2d) p. 84, Lacourciere, Judge (orally) (Ont. H.C.).

Another thing I did when I became warden was to regulate or standardize cell furnishings. One day when I completed inmate cell inspections, I observed that some inmates had very few things in their cells. Other inmates' cells were clean, but had no extra cell furniture. I stopped at cell 23, "B" Range. I knew this was Marlene's cell. She was away at work in the beauty shop. When I looked into her cell, I could not believe my eyes. I observed that she had so much prison furniture in her cell that you could barely turn around. She had a small fish tank with a small fish (discarded from the school and used for biology class), an old, high hospital bed, bookshelves, one large dresser, two radios, two televisions, two or three toasters, numerous electrical cords, an extension cord plugged into the range wall, and lots of personal items removed from the beauty shop. I observed a shrine on her dresser, with small candles surrounding a picture of her only boy. It was readily apparent that staff were casting a blind eye when inspecting her cell.

The inmates on "B" range were all part of Marlene's gang. I am sure Marlene helped select new inmates for her smaller

Upper "B" Range.
(Author)

range. I suspected that some correctional supervisors might have received Marlene's blessings before a new inmate was selected to reside on "B" range.

I discussed the excessive furniture in Marlene's cell and the cells of two other inmates on "B" range. I directed security staff to remove extra cell furniture in ten to twelve cells in "A" and "B" ranges, in keeping with the fire code and inspection reports. In order to be fair, I did not remove all Marlene's cell belongings at once. Every few months, items were removed to meet fire concerns. Marlene was upset and did everything she could to undermine my authority. It was not easy for a young warden against this adversary, a hardened criminal and prison-wise inmate who controlled many tough, difficult inmates.

The longer I stayed as warden, the more it became clear to Marlene that her influence was being diminished month by month.

Sometimes I approached Marlene to resolve problems if the inmate committee was weak or ineffective. I remember in the spring of 1981 a large, sharp knife went missing from the kitchen after lunch was served. It was not on the shadow board, a method to control knives and special tools. I directed that all the inmates be locked in their cells until the knife was found. Staff searched the institution and found other homemade weapons, and drugs, but no large knife. A large, sharp knife was definitely a severe threat to staff and could be used as a weapon against another inmate. The inmates were locked up for two days. The pressure was getting to both staff and inmates alike. I received several delegations from concerned staff and religious visitors, and a representative of the Elizabeth Fry Society (an advocacy group for female offenders) lobbied to allow the inmates out of their cells. Three days hence, on Saturday, a family day had been scheduled for inmates to spend time with their loved ones and family members in the yard. Family days were very important to inmates. The main reason was visiting, but unfortunately a number of inmates took the opportunity to arrange for drugs to be smuggled into the prison.

On this occasion, I told Marlene that unless I received the knife, I had no other option but to cancel family day. I knew Marlene's son had been approved to complete his first visit and family day with her. She wanted the family day activity to go on as planned. Marlene spoke quickly from behind her cell bars. She said, "Warden, if I can locate the knife, will there be a charge?" I said, "If you find out where the knife is and we get it back, I will be satisfied with the return of the knife." At the time, the inmate committee was not strong, but the chair was okay. She was an intelligent drug addict from Vancouver, but she was a weak, ineffective executive. She resided in the wing where there were few hardened inmates.

I consulted with the AW Security. It was time to act. I allowed Marlene out of her cell in the morning to walk the ranges and talk to each inmate at her cell. No luck. At about two forty-five in the afternoon, Marlene approached a security officer and asked to see me in my office. Marlene was escorted to my office. When she entered, she asked for a smoke. She said, "If I tell you where the knife is, will you release the population and not cancel family day?"

I looked at her and said, "Positively."

Marlene reported that a new inmate had taken the knife for protection. Marlene told me the knife could be found under a drain tile near the main yard door entrance. I called security and had them check the drain tile near the outside yard. Within five minutes, I received a call from the security office. They had the knife. I expressed my thanks to Marlene for her help. I telephoned the AW Security and directed her to let the inmates out of their cells at three p.m., since we had the knife. I called the Chief of Social Development and said that Family Day was on. I telephoned the chief steward in the kitchen and said, "Please order in thirty-two large pizzas for dinner."

I did not forget Marlene's help in obtaining the knife. I gave the approval for Marlene to have a private family visit weekend, several months later, in the family visiting house with her son. Inmates that received the family visiting program prepared their own food and enjoyed playing cards and watching movies and television. Inmates selected their specific foods and movies for the weekend. In my opinion, the FVP was one of the best program activities that Correctional Service of Canada had developed. Marlene's life changed after that visit with her son.

Looking back, it was a difficult decision to lock down the institution for two and a half days, but it was necessary. Several years previously, two knives had been removed from a workshop. Within two days, two inmates were stabbed and had to be admitted to an outside hospital.

The most difficult part of locking up the institution was that many innocent, positive inmates had their daily visits cancelled. In my opinion, inmate visits are a positive program activity and the most important factor for an inmate's rehabilitation and change for the better.

I put a lot of pressure on myself, but I needed the knife. I don't know if I would really have cancelled the scheduled family day. Some inmates' families and loved ones travelled hundreds of miles to attend this event.

I consulted Marlene less and less each month. Finally, in 1983, Marlene realized that if she was to get out of the box (prison), she needed to appear positive and disengage herself from the most criminally minded inmates. Her visit with her son helped to change her. She had a reason to live. She had hope. Hope is a very important anchor for people.

One morning, Marlene asked to see me. When she entered my office, she requested a smoke. She looked straight into my eyes and said, "Caron, could you do me a favour?" She asked if she could have a room in "the wing." The wing was a more relaxed area of the prison. The inmates were more positive and planned on getting out of the institution. In the wing, inmates have their own rooms. Toilet and bathing activities were available in another separate room. She knew I could veto this request.

I looked at Marlene and said, "Okay, but I don't want any problems in the wing."

Within three weeks, several rooms became available in the wing area. Marlene was approved for the wing in 1983—twelve years after she was admitted to the prison.

Her hospital bed was the last prison item that was removed from her cell when she moved to the wing. Marlene's time was becoming difficult for her to manage. She had a son who was twenty-two years old. She wanted to get out and spend some time with him before she was too old.

In 1985, Marlene was allowed to take advantage of the escorted temporary day program to leave and visit her son. In 1986, the Parole Board granted Marlene unescorted passes to be with her son in Toronto. Before Christmas, Marlene was granted day parole to a halfway house in Toronto that was managed and supervised by the Elizabeth Fry Society. Marlene was prohibited from drinking alcohol. Marlene might take the odd drink, but I didn't really think she would be back. In 1987, Marlene was granted full parole.

Marlene's departure was the end of an era. In her day, Marlene had a considerable amount of informal power that affected how the prison ran. I was glad that I did not have too many run-ins with her. Looking back, I realize I had gained a new respect and appreciation for Murray White's methods in using all his props—including the Queen Bee—to run his institution effectively.

Private Family Visitation (PFV)

Eligible inmates were offered the opportunity to participate in private family visits.

The main purpose of the private visits was intended to support family relationships and provide separate facilities where they could meet privately with their families to renew and strengthen family relations.

In November 1981, the Prison for Women opened a modern, two-bedroom bungalow located inside the prison grounds. An eligible inmate could spend a few days of privacy with the family or by herself. Previous to this date, male inmates serving time in several institutions in the Kingston area had been enjoying family visits successfully and uneventfully for over twelve months.

The majority of applications were from inmates with children.

The newly constructed facility had a private area where an inmate could socialize with her family. The inmate and her guest(s) had freedom to use a small yard space enclosed by a three-metre chain-link fence.

The inmate pre-ordered and selected her food and movies for the weekend and prepared her own meals. The inmate and guest could play games, watch movies or television, play ping pong, play cards, and relax. If weather permitted, a barbecue was available for outdoor cooking.

An inmate had access to the institutional physician, and the two of them could decide what, if any, birth-control methods would be used.

A visit usually would start on Friday afternoon and end on Monday morning (a forty-three-hour duration). During the forty-three hours of privacy, the visit would be interrupted three times daily: twice by visiting correctional officers (they would telephone first), and once by the requirement that the inmate stand on the front steps to let guards know she was still present.

Eligibility

Generally, inmates were eligible for a PFV every three months, with the exception of those who were assessed as currently being at risk of becoming involved in violent family issues, or who had committed acts of violence against children. Inmates who received unescorted temporary absences for the purpose of family contact were not eligible. Inmates who had received convictions for serious disciplinary charges were usually denied participation for a period of time.

Common-law spouses were allowed to visit if they had lived with the inmate for at least six months before incarceration.

Security Screening

All inmates' visitors had to complete an application and information form for the purpose of security screening. On the basis of a security assessment, and following a review of possible restrictions, the warden would decide whether or not visitor clearance would be granted. Finally, a positive community assessment helped the warden to grant a visit.

In my opinion, the Private Visiting Program was one of the best program activities that Correctional Service of Canada has developed.

The Baseball Team

While touring the institution during the late spring, I observed the baseball team practising on the baseball diamond located on the southwest corner of the prison property. The playing field was in reasonable shape, although the bleachers needed repairs and painting. My mind slipped into reverse. I remembered 1975, when I arrived at the Prison for Women as a naive assistant warden responsible for inmate programs. I was a very sports-minded person. I had previously coached and played different sports, including baseball, football, and basketball. The PFW baseball team needed a coach. I mentioned to the warden that I was interested in coaching the team. He responded quickly. "You're hired!" As a new staff member, I was somewhat overwhelmed with the new job. Taking on coaching the ladies' fastball team was a daunting challenge.

The next day, I placed posters throughout the prison on all information boards advising inmates that there would be a team meeting tomorrow in the gym at 3:45 p.m. I spoke to the inmate committee members and advised "Klassy," the head of recreation.

Klassy was an older English lady with white hair who was always ready to help the inmates. She was an energetic person and was especially gifted when it involved arts and crafts. Klassy had an office near the gym area. When she found out I was going to coach the baseball team, she said, "Do you know what you are getting yourself into?"

I responded, "No, but I will learn."

The next day, I went to the gym at 3:45 p.m. Twenty inmates were willing to turn out for the team. I indicated that fifteen inmates would be selected. The following day, we hit the field at 3:35 p.m. It was obvious that the team needed a lot of work. Most of the players who had turned out were hard-core inmates, drug addicts, murderers, and thieves.

After one week of running the team very hard, five players either got hurt, quit, or realized they had no skill to play this game. During the following practice, I told the team we would be joining a women's city league that had six teams. The interest in the league was high.

Our team was very strong behind the plate. Joy was the catcher. She was a gifted, fearless player who could run, catch, and hit the ball very well. She was excellent at catching for our pitchers. Joy was a hardened, serious drug addict (heroin) from Vancouver. She had very large hands and powerful legs. She was extremely strong and could throw a mean ball.

Our number one pitcher, Jo Ann, was excellent. She could throw a wicked curve ball. Pat was another heroin addict from the West Coast. She could play ball and enjoyed playing first base. Cathy played second base. She was a strong, muscular woman who was a loud-mouthed homosexual. She made it known that she liked females. Third base was played by April, a twenty-six-year-old black woman. April's play was either hot or cold. You never knew how she would play during a game. Diane played shortstop. She was a twenty-eight-year-old lifer for murder. Marlene, a twenty-seven-year-old Native girl from BC serving a life sentence, played centre field. She was our fastest player and could run down many fly balls. She ran like a deer. The other two out-field positions were shared between four players. Our backup pitchers were good for one or two innings. If we lost our starting pitcher for any reason, we would be in trouble.

The team worked hard and improved. We played our first game on Monday night.

We won 10–5. By the fifth week, the team had 5 wins and 0 losses. On game night, many inmates and some staff came to watch the game. The majority of the inmates who came to the games were lesbians. A number of very loud and aggressive inmates embarrassed me. They taunted the other team, calling them names. The umpire had to speak several times, asking the fans to calm down and leave out the nasty words.

Each game we played was a surprise to me. I never knew from week to week which players would be available. Some inmates would be stoned, or placed in segregation, or in the hospital, or out on a temporary absence pass. At the end of the season, we finished in first place. We won our first playoff game, winning 4–2, and reached the finals. On August 6, I felt reasonably confident that we had a good shot to win the cup.

At game time I put the strongest players on the field. The players were dropping balls left and right. Our number one pitcher was hit hard, balls being hit all over the field. By the end of the 4th inning, I was sitting down at the end of the bench. We were losing 5–3. I could not believe my eyes. We were making numerous mistakes. We lost the game 7–4.

There was something different about the team. I felt bad. I don't like to lose. Three months later, Diane approached me in the gym and said it was not my fault we lost the final game. I responded, "What do you mean?" Diane stated that one inmate's friend brought drugs in on the family day and shared them with many inmates on the team, including her. Most of the team members were stoned the day of the game. I learned a lot about the inmates during that summer. I realized that there were no perfect inmates or staff at the PFW.

One afternoon several weeks later, I was advised by the AW Security that four new inmates had arrived in Kingston by air. Two escort vehicles with four security staff members and two drivers were sent to the airport to pick up the four inmates and their personal belongings and relevant inmate files. At 4:14 p.m., the four inmates were admitted into the institution. It was mid-August and relatively mild outside. The Chief of Health Care reviewed the medical files and verified that all inmates were free of infectious disease. One inmate was placed on "A" range (the largest range in the prison), while the other three were placed in segregation. Mary Ann (of the mouse tattoo) was placed in protective custody in a cell located on the second-floor tier, and the two Doukhobor inmates were placed in segregation. Within minutes, the two Doukhobor leaders were talking Russian-Doukhobor language to the other seven inmates held in the segregation area.

2

Mary Ann's First Week in the Prison for Women

The next morning, I interviewed Mary Ann. I asked her how her first night had been. Mary Ann commented that she had to get used to the noise from the cell doors being opened and closed. She stated she did not know any of the other six inmates in protective custody. Although I had read Mary Ann's file, I wanted to hear her story in her own words. She opened up and spoke freely. She told me that she had been sentenced to life after removing a newborn baby from the maternity floor at St. Mary's Hospital in the Vancouver area.

After telling me that she had stolen a baby, Mary Ann seemed a bit apprehensive while telling me the rest of her story. Mary Ann explained that she left Canada and travelled to San Francisco. I asked Mary Ann, "Why did you return to San Francisco?"

Mary Ann responded convincingly, "I missed my children. I needed to see them and ensure they were all right." Mary Ann's drive to return to her children's birthplace was like a robin returning to my grass-covered field each spring.

I asked Mary Ann, "Can you tell me why you took the baby from the hospital?"

There was a long pause and silence. Small tear droplets oozed out of her eyes like a spring rain and fell to the floor, spattering on the papers lying on the floor. Agonizing pain seemed to reach Mary Ann's soul. She began to cry. "I miss having little children near me. I can't breathe without them. I am dead, like a corpse in a casket." She cried uncontrollably. Given her extreme vulnerability, I backed away from the cell bars.

Looking back, perhaps it was wrong to ask sensitive questions at this time, but I felt Mary Ann needed to relieve the pain in her heart. Many months later, Mary Ann thanked me for helping her relieve the guilt and pain she had felt for her selfish act of removing a baby from the hospital. Mary Ann ended by saying that she trusted me and had never really told her complete story to anyone before.

I told Mary Ann that she would be assigned to the school program, and later that day she could expect an interview from her classification officer. Initially, the classification supervisor stated he would handle her case until his most experienced classification officer returned from his holidays in three weeks. He was aware that Mary Ann was a very insecure girl who lacked self-esteem.

During the next couple of weeks, the AW Security received daily reports from her security staff that Mary Ann was fitting in okay in the PC unit. The schoolteacher, who was aware of Mary Ann's fragile background, signed her up for Grade 8 and 9 lesson plans.

After the first six weeks, I observed that Mary Ann was getting friendly with two of the other inmates in the PC unit. One of the inmates had strangled her child in a drunken rage after a fight with her boyfriend. The little girl survived. The Children's Aid Society removed the child from the inmate's custody. One Friday afternoon, this inmate, whose name was Tanya, received two negative communications. First, Tanya was denied day parole in the early afternoon. The Parole Board said that she was not ready to return to the community. Inexplicably, in the late afternoon Tanya received a telephone call from the Children's Aid worker in Edmonton telling her that her child had died from complications from her injuries. Tanya went bananas. She cried out loud and presented a liturgy of profanities against the world. Tanya became very depressed and shouted that she did not want to live. Her extreme rage disrupted the entire unit. Tanya was removed to the hospital and placed under the doctor's care. The minister and psychologist were called to help this inmate. Solace and dead silence filled the PC unit. A caring guard reported to me that all the inmates went to their cells and cried.

When I toured the PC unit at approximately four-thirty p.m., Mary Ann was very upset that her friend had received such bad news. Mary Ann started to cry and said that she could not talk to anyone today. I agreed to see her on Monday morning.

When interviewed, Mary Ann opened up. She said, "Mr. Caron, I don't know if I can live in this environment. There is so much hurt and pain." I indicated that she would have better days. She asked me if I had a cigarette. I sheepishly stated I only had a pack of filtered cigarettes. I kept a pack of smokes for exactly this reason. Mary Ann reached over and said, "Thank you, I need a smoke badly. I tried to quit, but smoking helps resolve the pressure in me." She took a big drag like it was her last cigarette on earth.

I informed her that the schoolteacher had advised me that she was doing very good work and had almost finished her first lesson plan for grades 8 and 9.

Mary Ann's Background Offence

I saw Mary Ann in the PC unit weekly and noticed some progress. I recall the first week in December. One day Mary Ann really opened up. I let her talk. She told me that she was born in New Mexico. Her mother and stepfather were mill workers. She was twenty-three years old and had left home when she was seventeen. Mary Ann felt compelled to push out her unhappy childhood memories. She said, "I did not get along with my stepfather. He drank too much. He became aggressive towards my mother when he became intoxicated. When I reached my teenage years, he tried to have sex with me but I was able to beat him off mainly because he was so drunk." She took two more big drags from her cigarette and remarked that she made sure she was never alone with him.

"Did your mother suspect anything?"

"I don't believe she did. I never had the guts to tell her."

Mary Ann opened up a large gusher. Her voice trembled as she spoke. She wanted the pain to leave her heart. She told me that she rode with her husband, seated behind him on his Harley Davidson motorcycle. Her husband's name was Willy. He was the leader of the San Francisco chapter of the Hell's Angels motorcycle gang. She had been exposed to poison in her life. She had witnessed criminal acts and lots of violence. Willy and Mary

Ann were together for five and half years. They had two children, Molly, age two, and John, age four. Willy pressured Mary Ann to have sex with other full patch (fully fledged) members. Mary Ann said she could not do what he asked her to do.

Looking back, Mary Ann remembered Willy going ballistic one night in Oakland. The club executive members attended a party where drugs and excessive alcohol were consumed. Willy approached Mary Ann in the bathroom and said, "Kid, it is necessary for you to have sex with Danny and Chief."

Mary Ann snapped back. "What? Are you kidding? I can't fuck these guys. I love you, but if you make me do this, I will leave you." Tears ran down her face like a waterfall in a small canyon. "I can't breathe. I have to get out of here." Mary Ann went outside and walked for several blocks. Willy was so loaded that he did not remember her leaving. She caught a taxi and went home.

The next day, the tension in their home was unbearable. Willy, still high on drugs, grabbed Mary Ann and fucked her without her consent. "Listen, bitch, I need you to fuck Danny and Chief. My leadership depends on it." Mary Ann grabbed a whisky bottle, drank it all, and fell into unconsciousness.

Mary Ann said she could not do what her husband wanted. Willy threatened her and said that if she did not fuck the two gang members, he would make it difficult for her.

Several days later, in mid-1979, Mary Ann decided to leave with the clothes on her back. Willy told her he would hurt her bad if she left him. Furthermore, if she did not do what he asked, he would make sure that she could not see her children.

Mary Ann was extremely upset. She explained that she was scared to tell anyone that she was leaving. She trembled as tears were released from her eyes. This situation caused her great pain. Mary Ann mentioned that she borrowed some money from an old friend and caught a bus to Canada. She had seen a poster of Vancouver and it caught her attention. Mary Ann pointed out that she loved her children and it was difficult to leave them, but she feared for her life.

When the bus got near the Canadian border, Mary Ann's heart started to pound. She started to sweat profusely. She was wound up like a jack in a box. The bus stopped at the border crossing.

The door to the bus opened. The border agent walked down the aisle checking each passenger's identification. Mary Ann remembered that she was so nervous, she had peed her pants.

The border agent asked, "Where were you born?"

"New Mexico."

He continued, "What brings you to Canada?"

"I am going to Vancouver to visit Stanley Park and the zoo. I love killer whales."

Suddenly, the agent said, "Welcome to Canada!"

The bus sped off, leaving a large plume of smoke. Mary Ann arrived in Vancouver at seven o'clock on Tuesday night. She found a cheap hotel downtown (weekly rate). The next day, she started to look for employment by reading the local newspapers. She was lucky; an opening had occurred in the nursery of a nearby hospital. A nursing health aide had been involved in a serious car accident and would be off for several months.

Mary Ann walked up to the personnel office in Saint Mary's Hospital. She took the elevator to the seventh floor. When she exited the elevator, Mary Ann saw a sign that read "Human Resources Turn to the Left."

Mary Ann walked into the office. "I am here to apply for the job advertised in the Vancouver newspaper."

The young clerk, who was chewing gum, looked up at Mary Ann and said, "Which position?"

"I am interested in the health-care aide position for the nursery program."

The clerk sat back in her chair and spat out the gum from her chubby cheeks. "Did you know that the position is only for four months?"

"No, but that is okay."

The clerk explained that the incumbent was injured in a car accident and would be off for four months. The clerk handed Mary Ann some application forms that needed to be filled out. "Please fill out all three sheets and return them to me. There is a spare room across the hall."

Mary Ann filled out the forms and noticed line 10 in the main form. Line 10 asked for related experience. Mary Ann thought about it for a few seconds and put down that she had worked at Mercy Hospital in San Francisco for three years, until 1978 when she moved away from a broken marriage. Mary Ann recorded that she had worked in the maternity ward, including the nursery, feeding and cleaning babies.

When Mary Ann returned the application forms to the clerk, a nurse supervisor walked into the room. "Good morning," she said.

The clerk told the older nurse that Mary Ann was there for the nursing aide position. The older nurse, who had just come from the maternity ward, said they were already short two staff in the unit. "Two staff members are home with the 'flu." The nurse, who wore dark glasses, reviewed Mary Ann's application and said, "I see you worked at Mercy Hospital for three years."

"Yes, I worked in the nursery room."

"Good." The nurse turned around and said, "Miss Harkness, could you start tomorrow?"

"Yes, I could."

The nurse responded, "Do you have any problem with taking a 'flu shot?"

"No."

"Great! Please report to room 705 in twenty minutes. They will sign you up. By the way, you are aware the job is only for four months?"

"Yes, I am aware of that."

"Tomorrow, report at seven a.m. to Ms. Brooks. She is the nurse in charge of the nursery."

"Thank you for the opportunity. I won't let you down."

Shortly after leaving the hospital, Mary Ann's heart was beating like a large drum. She smoked four cigarettes in a row. She remembered smoking herself silly.

Mary Ann went back to her hotel room and celebrated her good fortune. She had two beers and set the portable alarm for 5:30 a.m. In case she did not wake up, she asked the hotel clerk to wake her at 6:00 a.m. The hospital was only an eighteen-minute walk away. She had a good night's sleep.

Mary Ann remembered that she awoke at 5:15 a.m. She was in the shower when her alarm went off. She made herself a coffee and toast in a small room near the office and then headed for her new job. The outside temperature was around sixty-nine degrees. A little mist filled the air.

Mary Ann stated that she was determined to make her job a success. She arrived at the hospital at 6:45 a.m. She took the elevator to the tenth floor, where the maternity and nursery facilities were located. Next to the nursery there were two separate rooms where premature babies were being cared for and another secure room where specialized doctors and nurses cared for six very sick babies in incubators. These babies had received medical procedures and major surgery, such as heart operations; some had serious breathing problems.

Mary Ann approached a young nurse and asked where she could find Nurse Brooks. She was sent down the hall into a small office. Nurse Brooks was a recent graduate with a Masters in Nursing Science from the University of British Columbia. She had a cap on her head that read "RCH." Later, she would find out that Nurse Brooks had studied nursing at the Royal Columbian Hospital in New Westminster and graduated in 1961.

Nurse Brooks was known as "Bubbles." She was a heavy-set woman who had bright red hair and scores of freckles on her face and hands. She ran the nursery program. "Welcome aboard," said Ms. Brooks. Mary Ann filled out some more papers and was given her hospital identification card and white coat to cover her street clothes. "You can wear white pants and a shirt." Mary Ann told Ms. Brooks that she left California to escape a bad marriage. Ms Brooks advised Mary Ann that she could obtain a white nurse's uniform across the street in a little shop.

"Come with me." Ms. Brooks took Mary Ann to a room near the nursery. There were two other nursing aide workers in the room, and Mary Ann was introduced to them. Ms. Brooks explained that this week Mary Ann would be cleaning milk bottles and feeding babies. Next week, Mary Ann would be washing diapers and cleaning the sleeping areas.

Mary Ann watched the other nursing aides like a hawk. After several hours, she appeared to be performing the job like an experienced employee. Mary Ann was apprehensive because she had had no formal experience or training in looking after babies.

At the end of the first week, Ms. Brooks stated that the lady that completed reference checks was away for four weeks because of a family illness. Mary Ann felt nervous, but did not comment.

Six weeks later, Ms. Brown appeared in the nursing station and advised Ms. Brooks that she was going to check the reference given by Mary Ann and that of a new nurse. Ms. Brooks said, "Check the reference for the nurse. I believe Mary Ann Harkness is okay, so forget about her reference check until you get back from your knee operation." Ms. Brown had scheduled surgery and would be off for three months.

Mary Ann remarked that she did an excellent job in the nursery and was given more responsibilities. After two months' work experience, a nurse sometimes would ask Mary Ann to carry babies down to the discharge area on the first floor.

One night, Mary Ann telephoned a friend in San Francisco who lived near her former house. The friend told Mary Ann that her children were living with Willy's mother in a house close to the Golden Gate Bridge until the end of August, at which time they would go to his sister's house in Sacramento. Mary Ann thanked the woman and told her that she was in Nevada and missed the kids. Her friend said that she would not tell anyone that she had called.

During the early morning of the next day, in her seventh week of employment, Mary Ann became depressed and missed her children dearly. She had saved $1,500 dollars and enjoyed her job. Socially, Mary Ann had formed a relationship with another nursing aide worker.

Then Mary Ann broke down and cried. She felt guilty. She admitted that she became attached to a little baby girl born four days previously. The mother of the baby had three-year-old twin girls and a six-year-old boy at home. Mary Ann liked the mother but said few words to her. Mary Ann adored the baby.

The next day, Mary Ann had a difficult time bringing the baby to her mother for feeding. She explained that she did not understand what was happening to her emotions. She carried the little baby girl to her mother, who tried to breastfeed the infant. Mary Ann said, "I will pick up the baby in one hour."

Mary Ann picked up the baby after one hour and returned the child to the nursery. After she left work that day, her mind went crazy. She wanted to see her children in San Francisco. She was fearful that if her children were moved to Sacramento she might not see them again. Mary Ann wanted a child. She felt a baby would fill her void. She did not believe she would see her children again.

Mary Ann emphasized that she had a very difficult night. She wrestled with her thoughts. Her mind raced forward and in reverse. "Child, children gone"; "I need help." Mary Ann was overwhelmed with her situation. She knew the little baby she loved would be leaving the next day.

Mary Ann recalled that the next morning everything appeared normal at work. She remembered that at 10:45 a.m. her supervisor asked her to get baby Richards ready for discharge. According to Mary Ann, everything seemed normal until she picked up the baby girl to go downstairs to the discharge area on the main floor.

The new mother had already been escorted down to the discharge area. It would take fifteen to twenty minutes for the mother to be processed, depending on how busy they were. Mary Ann agreed to carry the baby down to the car after the mother completed her discharge papers.

Mary Ann stressed that she had worked there for two and a half months and had received excellent performance reports. She was trusted. Mary Ann told me she began to tremble. She started to feel guilty. Then she said, "I did it."

"What do you mean?"

She had a sudden urge to leave with the baby. Mary Ann dressed the baby and placed her wallet, sweater, and pants under the blanket. She then took off the baby's hospital identification wristband. She walked to the elevator. Her heart was racing. She entered the elevator and pushed the down buttons for the first and 3rd floors. Two floors down (8th floor), the door opened. She trembled. A skinny male orderly got onto the elevator. He pressed the 5th floor button and the door opened. Mary Ann related that she grabbed the elevator door with one hand and exited the elevator. She walked down the stairs of the hospital and left the building at the back door. She remembered walking quickly for two or three blocks and then got on a city bus and travelled for about five miles. She reached the bus station and exited the bus. She was absolutely compelled to take the baby to California.

I asked her, "Did you think of the baby's mother?"

Mary Ann made no eye contact with me. She seemed dead inside. She appeared to be in a trance with no facial expression. She reported that she reached the bus station one minute before a bus was to depart for White Rock, British Columbia, a small town near the Canada/Washington border.

Mary Ann took a big drag on her cigarette and continued. She reported that she met a trucker from Oregon in a small café and asked him for help. "I am leaving Vancouver to escape an abusive husband." She looked straight into the trucker's brown eyes and asked him point blank, "Will you help me to get across the border? I don't want my husband to know I entered the USA. He wants the baby. Will you hide me in the sleeping quarters? I will give the baby a sleeping pill to help her sleep when crossing the border."

The truck driver was reluctant to offer help. Mary Ann used her charm and said there was something in it for him in Seattle. She implied sexual favours. The trucker agreed after getting a long kiss and a touch of her breast. Mary Ann shopped briefly at a nearby grocery store and bought several items, including baby bottles, diapers, and some milk.

They arrived in Seattle about three hours later during a rainstorm. The trucker experienced motor problems with his rig. He could not go any further until he had his truck engine repaired. Mary Ann agreed to meet him at the Holiday Inn near the highway in Portland, Oregon, two days later. The trucker gave Mary Ann $350 for expenses in exchange for her wedding ring.

Mary Ann never saw the trucker again. She got on a bus and travelled to Mount Shasta, California. She stayed overnight in small motel and the next morning took the bus to San Francisco, arriving the following day. When the trucker returned to Vancouver, he saw Mary Ann's face on television. The trucker told police that he had picked up a hitchhiker with a baby near Bellingham, Washington, and had driven her to Seattle. He said she looked very similar to the woman on television.

The Vancouver police alerted the police in California and Oregon. They forwarded Mary Ann's picture to the San Francisco police. Within two days, Mary Ann was arrested at a small motel. She was extradited and escorted back to Canada by police within three months. The baby was returned immediately to Vancouver to be united with her parents. Mary Ann went to court and received a life sentence for kidnapping the baby. She was eligible for parole in seven years.

After Mary Ann told her story, she cried and cried. She said, "Warden, I am so sorry for what I have done. I want to change my life." Mary Ann indicated that tonight she would write a letter to the baby's mother and father asking for their forgiveness. I stated that it was the right thing to do.

"Mouse, it will help to heal your pain." (This was the first time I had called Mary Ann by her nickname.)

Attempted Escape

The months went fast. Soon it was Christmastime again, 1981.

One of the goals or desires of many inmates is the dream of escaping custody. Inmate escapes or attempted escapes in the seventies and eighties were more common than correctional officials cared to report. During my tenure in management, no inmate ever successfully escaped over the fence (I started in 1975). We had, however, a number of close calls. In 1974, two inmates escaped over the old sixteen-foot wall by climbing a tree and jumping over it. In 1973, one inmate hid herself in a truck and left the prison at the sally port exit, the area where large vehicles entered the prison to bring in supplies and equipment.

One day in late 1970, two inmates attempted to scale the new eighteen-foot reinforced concrete wall. They were almost successful. One inmate was close to the top of the wall, but a rope she was using snapped. She fell on the second inmate, who was below her. One inmate broke her leg, and the second inmate broke her arm. Both were found guilty and received an additional eighteen months to their sentence.

PFW Old Wall, 1960.
(Courtesy Corrections Service Canada Museum)

The new wall, 1980.
(Courtesy Corrections
Service Canada
Museum)

In the early fall of 1981, staff intercepted a major escape plot. A Quebec inmate who had been convicted of first-degree murder and sentenced to life with no parole for twenty-five years, wrote a note to her boyfriend in Quebec outlining the details of her escape plan. The inmate in question, Josee, had been a strip dancer at a night club in Hull, Quebec. Josee was a very attractive twenty-eight-year-old woman with long, blonde hair and large, firm breasts. She was a sexy woman who used her assets well.

I clearly remember the day Josee arrived at the prison. It was about eleven forty-five a.m. when I looked outside my window and observed two Quebec Provincial Police cars driving up to the front of the prison. Four heavily armed police officers with side revolvers, rifles, and a shotgun exited the cars. My eyes were glued on their prize. The police were escorting Josee to the prison. A few minutes before, the police had escorted a high-profile male inmate and deposited him at Kingston Penitentiary, located a short distance down the street. Josee was handcuffed and wearing leg irons. She walked awkwardly from side to side like a penguin as she slowly approached the front stairs. The scene was unreal. I don't recall ever seeing such strong police presence for one inmate. The Quebec police were very concerned that Josee's gang members would attempt to assist her to escape from custody. Josee was involved with a gang of high-level gangsters. Her boyfriend was the leader of the gang.

The large oak doors to the prison opened. Once they were inside the front hall, the large, metal, electronic doors opened with considerable noise. Josee was escorted into the foyer. The police removed her handcuffs and leg irons. The Inmate Sentence Administrator reviewed the documents and admitted Josee to her new home. The police exited the prison. Josee passed through another metal electronic door before she was escorted into the belly of the prison. I am sure the opening and closing of the large metal doors had a deliberate impact on all new inmates arriving at the Prison for Women. It was a rite of passage for all imperfect people entering the institution.

Early one morning when the inmates were at a medical clinic, the Institutional Preventive Security Officer (IPSO) received word that Josee was planning to escape. The IPSO searched Josee's cell and found a letter dated the night before and ready for mailing out of the institution. The IPSO photocopied the note and returned it to its hiding place inside a Bible.

The note stated that Josee had a medical appointment with a specialist at Hotel Dieu Hospital on October 2 at one p.m. Josee asked her boyfriend, Pierre, to arrange for two members of his gang to come to Kingston. One member was to drive the getaway car. The second member was to dress up like a Franciscan priest. Two guns would be concealed under the priest's cassock. The gang member with the guns would take the doctor hostage until Josee was out of the building and in the car. The gunman would join Josee and the driver in a nearby parking lot. Once outside the city, the small car would be driven into a large transport truck, thereby concealing it. The truck would travel to Eastern Quebec near a small airport. A small float plane would fly to northern Quebec. The plane would land near Mt. Saint Marie on a small lake. After four weeks, the trio would travel by float plane to a location near Cornwall, Ontario. A small boat would take the trio into the USA. Forged passports and identification papers would be arranged. The plan was very detailed. Once Pierre received the note, he was to send a letter to Josee telling her that he was buying a small yellow convertible. This was the password indicating that the escape was on. The IPSO arranged for the plan to be shared with the RCMP, the Kingston City Police, and the Ontario Provincial Police (OPP).

On the day of the medical appointment, Josee was locked in segregation. The police were waiting for the disguised priest. Before one p.m., the disguised priest was captured in the parking lot before he could enter the hospital. He was found with no guns but did have counterfeit passports and identification papers for Josee and the gang members. The gang member who had dressed up like a priest was taken to a provincial jail. Several weeks later, he died in hospital after suffering a heart attack. The second gang member who was the car driver was never found. He escaped with guns and lots of cash.

We were lucky to intercept this note. It is quite possible Josee would have made good her escape attempt. The OPP and RCMP worked with the Quebec Provincial Police to place surveillance on the gang in Hull, Quebec. Josee was not charged with any additional offences. It seemed as though she would remain at the PFW for many years. In 1988, Josee was transferred to a female prison in Quebec.

Mary Ann's Second Christmas

The weeks seemed to go by quickly for staff. Inmates, on the other hand, found that the weeks and months went by slowly. Mary Ann continued to work really hard on her education. She told me that she would stay up late at night and work on her assignments. Sometimes she would be up until four a.m. The teacher praised Mary Ann, telling her that she was one of the most motivated students in the prison. Mary Ann continued to make great progress in the PC Unit; in fact, she appeared to be one of the leaders.

The days in December disappeared. Soon Mary Ann was celebrating her second Christmas at the prison. I remember the Salvation Army representatives bringing small bags of goodies for the inmates in segregation. Mary Ann and the other inmates in PC were so appreciative to receive some small personal items. Mary Ann received no visits or mail. It was like she had fallen into a deep hole and no one knew where she was. I continued to encourage her, telling her that 1982 would be a good year for her.

Inappropriate Relationships

As the months passed, there were always events that occurred that required my attention. Given the loneliness and despair that some inmates experienced without the presence of loved ones or family to help balance their lives, the need for affection grew greatly. Sometimes inmates became romantically involved with staff. During my tenure as warden, I encountered four employees that crossed the line and got involved with an inmate. Two staff when confronted admitted their love for an inmate and resigned. One employee was fired, and another was transferred out of the prison and reassigned to Regional Headquarters.

In 1979, I received information from inmate sources advising me that a psychologist was having an affair with an inmate named Helen. This was a seriously sensitive allegation that required close attention and prudence. After receiving three separate confidential verbal reports from inmates within two weeks, including a discussion with a former chairperson of the Inmate Committee who shared their concerns, I knew I had to act. The reports continued to strongly suggest that the psychologist was involved with a certain attractive twenty-seven-year-old white female serving seven years for importation of drugs.

This confidential matter was discussed with the AW Security, AW Inmate Programs, and the AW Administration. The psychologist and inmate were watched very closely, but we could not obtain sufficient evidence to confront the psychologist.

One month later, Helen submitted a request for an escorted temporary absence (TA) pass to attend a specialized medical clinic and an AA (Alcoholics Anonymous) meeting in the community. The escort was the psychologist. The pass was to take effect in two weeks. The TA was discussed with the IPSO, AW Security, AW Inmate Programs, and the AW Administration. The decision was to approve the TA. The day the TA was granted, the psychologist was to return the inmate at 7:30 p.m. At 7:45 p.m., the psychologist telephoned the institution and stated he had car problems and would be back by 10:15 p.m. When the psychologist returned to the institution with the inmate, two staff members reported that the psychologist smelled of alcohol.

The following morning, I had the psychologist report to my office. The AW Administration and the AW Security were present. The psychologist was advised that we had evidence that he was having an affair with Helen. I told the psychologist that he had two choices: he could resign or he could be terminated. The psychologist asked to speak to Helen alone. Helen was called to my office. After five minutes, the psychologist advised me that he would submit a letter of resignation. The psychologist stated that he loved Helen. He requested permission to visit Helen on a regular basis, which was granted. Three months later, Helen was granted day parole. She eventually received a full parole. The psychologist married Helen one year later.

The following year, I encountered another inappropriate relationship between a staff member and an inmate. This was an incident involving a very attractive, dark-haired, twenty-six-year-old recreation officer who was responsible for recreation activities in the gymnasium area and outside exercise classes. It was not uncommon to find Mrs. Weaton in the gymnasium day or night with several inmates at her side. Mrs. Weaton had two assistants. One older woman from Poland was a cleaner. The second assistant was a twenty-nine-year-old white woman named Nancy who was very athletic and in great physical shape. She was Mrs. Weaton's recreational helper.

It seemed that every time I toured the gymnasium area, I saw Mrs. Weaton and Nancy together. Nancy was a very aggressive, determined lesbian who had had relationships with several attractive inmates during her four-year sentence. Her last relationship had ended five weeks previously, when her partner was released on parole to Western Canada. Nancy was in her last year of her sentence. She applied for parole and hoped to be released in two months.

One day, seven weeks later, I received a visit from Klassy, the recreational supervisor and Mrs. Weaton's boss. Klassy was somewhat nervous and had a difficult time speaking.

I said, "Klassy, what is on your mind?"

Klassy spoke quickly. "One of the inmates that I have a good relationship with told me that Mrs. Weaton and Nancy are having an inappropriate relationship. It seems that one inmate surprisingly caught them together in one of the backrooms of the gym in a sexual encounter. Apparently both women had removed their clothes."

I thanked Klassy and told her to lock the backrooms up and not give the key to anyone. I asked her to keep me informed. I discussed this matter with the AW Security and the AW Inmate Programs and asked that they monitor the situation.

Two weeks later, Nancy received parole to live in the community while she attended Saint Lawrence College. She had some money and rented an apartment. One afternoon, I received a call from Klassy asking to see me. Klassy told me that Mrs. Weaton had quit her job, left her husband, and was now living with Nancy. It was a difficult situation. Mrs. Weaton had been married to an army officer. Apparently he was completely surprised that his wife had left him.

It was not the last inappropriate relationship between staff and inmates that I had to deal with.

The Doukhobors

During the first part of 1982, Mary Ann had completed all outstanding courses for Grade 12. She was happy to start work on her Grade 13 assignments. As Mary Ann was proceeding full steam ahead, other problems were unfortunately emerging in the institution.

Generally, the Doukhobor inmates presented few problems, since they continued to reside in segregation. Two Doukhobor inmates completed their sentence and were released on Mandatory Supervision to Creston, British Columbia. During the first week in April, we had an incident with one of the two leaders of the Doukhobor inmates. Somehow Marta B., while waiting to see the doctor, obtained some matches from an inmate cleaner who worked in the hospital. Marta B. returned to her cell and during the night she started a small fire in her cell. Using toilet paper to start the fire, Marta was able to burn her sheets and her pyjamas. The correctional officers rushed to her cell and put out the small fire. Marta stood in her cell and recited a Russian–Doukhobor prayer. I was called at home and advised of the incident. I didn't realize at the time that this was the start of a long journey into hell.

The next night, three of the Doukhobor inmates threw everything in their cells except their blankets through the bars onto the range floor. They somehow got matches and burned toilet paper and their pyjamas, and threw them into the hallway floor. They also kept their blankets. Oddly, other inmates in segregation started yelling and throwing their personal items into the hallway corridor. Several inmates started throwing urine and feces as correctional officers walked by. It took staff three hours to clean up the mess and gain control of the situation. The inmates finally went to sleep at 3:30 a.m.

The next day, the Doukhobor inmates started to sing their songs together. Something was agitating them. They were becoming difficult to manage. Two days later, Marta B.'s and Molly A.'s husbands appeared in the afternoon at the front door of the prison and asked to visit their wives. I discussed their request with the senior staff. I agreed to allow closed visits in the visiting and correspondence room after three p.m. The husbands had come a long way and were concerned after they had received no communication from their wives. The two younger Doukhobor inmates that were released two months ago had probably given them a complete briefing.

The visit of the two Doukhobor men seemed to help. The Doukhobor inmates settled down and presented no problems for several months.

"A" Side, or South Cell Block.

(Courtesy Corrections Service Canada Museum)

New Inmates and a Business Proposal

There are so many small stories and events happening in a prison that sometimes it is difficult to keep up. During my tenure as warden, I encountered a number of firsts. I vividly remember the first week in May 1982. We received three new inmates from Toronto West Detention Centre. When possible, I tried to personally interview all new inmates within a day or two of their admission into the prison. One Tuesday morning, I was informed by the Inmate Sentence Administrator that three new inmates would arrive at the prison early the next day. At eleven a.m. the next day we actually received four new inmates. The fourth inmate had withdrawn her appeal and wanted to get her sentence started.

I interviewed the first two inmates before two p.m. They were both older and were convicted of fraud and drug activities. Both inmates, who had lengthy criminal records, exhibited numerous tattoos. These two inmates knew the drill and asked no questions. They were both returned to "A" range within minutes.

The third inmate was called to my office. When the door opened, I was completely taken aback. The inmate, named Angie, was a twenty-four-year-old dancer charged with her first sentence for drug possession. Angie was five foot nine inches tall, had long, blonde hair, and possessed beautiful facial features. She was an extremely attractive woman with a striking figure. Angie had large, firm breasts that were her greatest assets. I realized right away that the lesbian inmates in the population would immediately seek her attention. I tried to protect and warn Angie by saying that because of her good looks she would be targeted by aggressive homosexual inmates. I suggested that she pick her friends wisely.

Angie responded, "Don't worry about me, Warden. I am heterosexual and not interested in being with women."

I wished her good luck in completing her sentence at the prison. Angie had a Grade 12 education, but needed two courses to receive her diploma.

When Angie left my office, I was convinced that she could handle herself. She was assigned to "A" range, where the majority of difficult inmates resided. The next morning, I was making my rounds in the prison and I observed Angie walking near the classification office. I was completely surprised at what I saw. I noticed Angie's neck. It was full of hickies, perhaps suggesting she may have been involved in sexual activity with another inmate during the night. Later the same day, I saw Angie with Carole, a thirty-eight-year-old hard-core lesbian drug addict.

I was convinced Angie was involved with Carole, not because of sexual attraction, but because Carole could give her drugs in exchange for sexual favours. Several weeks later, I was informed that Angie was very intoxicated and had to be taken to segregation. Angie told an older, trusted correctional officer that she was giving sex for cocaine and other drugs. She admitted to being a hopeless drug addict. Angie, who was a first-time offender, was released on full parole one year later. I later learned that Angie overdosed on drugs in Toronto four months after receiving parole. Her body was found in an abandoned drug house. The police found her with a needle in her arm and drug paraphernalia near her body. A young woman with great potential had died prematurely.

The fourth inmate I interviewed was Sonyia. She was a forty-two-year-old Slavic woman, tall and attractive. Sonyia was very intelligent and in control of herself. As a first-time offender, Sonyia had received a three-year, six-month sentence for drug importation. Sonyia was cautioned that she might be approached because of her good looks and nice figure.

Sonyia laughed, "I am married to a doctor and I am not interested in such things. I can handle myself." Sonyia was a woman of means and she let you know it.

The next morning, I saw Sonyia coming down the staircase from "B" range, where she was assigned a cell. Right beside her was "Mugsy," a large Native Cree inmate from western Canada who used her muscles to get what she wanted. Mugsy was walking in lockstep with Sonyia. I could not figure out the relationship. Mugsy was basically illiterate, poor, and adversely affected by much abuse in her life. Sonyia was educated, intelligent, wealthy, and very self-confident.

One week later, Sonyia requested an interview with me in my office. Sonyia walked in and briefly looked out the window to the street in front of the prison. I suspected her mind was centred on the free people walking by the prison. Before I could say anything, Sonyia spoke. "I know it looks bad, Warden, but I am not involved with Mugsy. I agreed to pay her five dollars per week for protection from hard-core lesbians and other toughs in the prison." I didn't comment. I understood her predicament. She was determined to complete her sentence and return to Toronto.

Sonyia then sat down and made a request that I never expected. Sonyia told me she had an import/export business that imported mainly olive oil and dates from Lebanon and North Africa. She had ten staff members working for her business in Toronto. Her husband was a doctor and had no time to run her business. She said, "My business takes in $25,000 per week." She further remarked, "I don't need a job here in the kitchen or cleaning floors."

Sonyia went on. "Can I talk openly? The drug possession charge was not my fault. One of my employees, an illegal immigrant from Africa with a small baby, arranged for drugs to be brought into Canada using my shipping cans. I saved her life. I agreed to plead guilty of the possession charge. The original charge was for trafficking, but there was no evidence. I was told by my lawyer that I would get three years because of the small amount of drugs and being a first-time offender. My lawyer advised me that the woman (Shasa) responsible for the drugs would be married to a Canadian man within days and should receive her Canadian papers within six months. As soon as Shasa receives her Canadian papers, she will tell authorities that she was responsible for taking drugs into Canada to pay for medicine for her ill baby. Shasa is not a drug user and her prospects for being a responsible Canadian citizen are good."

Sonyia stressed that her business was legitimate and very profitable, and that she did not use drugs and never would. Her husband also did not use drugs.

After spending two hours with Sonyia, I was totally convinced that she was not a drug user and that she did indeed have a business venture in Toronto.

Sonyia looked at me and requested point blank something I never encountered before.

She said, "I want to run my business affairs from here. My husband would come weekly and discuss my business activities with me. I am prepared to open an account in the prison so that my financial dealings are processed in prison. I will take a salary of $3,000 per month." At first, I thought that her business dealings somehow might be involved with organized crime. Before leaving, Sonyia asked that I keep our conversation confidential and away from other inmates. I told her that I would look into the matter and get back to her.

Before she left my office I commented, "Please submit to me your business plan and how it would work in the prison."

I called a special meeting of the assistant wardens of finance, administration, inmate programs, and security. They were all skeptical but said it could work.

After I received Sonyia's business plan and her official request, I referred the matter to the security administrator at our Regional Headquarters. He in turn requested various police agencies, including the RCMP, OPP, City of Toronto police, and Interpol to comment. After four weeks, the answer came back positive. The police had no concerns about Sonyia's business plan. I reviewed our commissioner's directives and there was a section that allowed an inmate in rare circumstances to operate a business. I must admit that this was the only time I ever had an inmate request to operate a business from prison.

After reviewing all the positive reports, including recommendations from my staff and regional headquarters, I submitted the complete package and request for a business to National Headquarters. The request would have to be approved by the Commissioner of Corrections. RHQ Security contacted the Canadian Security Intelligence Centre (CSIC) and asked them for their views on this matter. To my surprise, CSIC and all the police forces had no objections to the plan. In three months, the Commissioner of Corrections approved the plan. I suspected that CSIC and the RCMP were going to watch this activity closely.

Sonyia operated her business openly. She opened an account and paid herself $3,000 per month. One of the assistant wardens remarked that she made more in one week than I made in a month. Sonyia's husband visited her weekly. He carried, in his briefcase, business papers that were searched by staff each time. In twelve months, Sonyia received a full parole.

In 1988, I met Sonyia by chance in a Birks Toronto Eaton Centre jewellery shop. She thanked me for my support for her business plan. She explained that after six years, her business was very successful and grossing five million dollars per year. She employed twenty people, including one inmate she met at the prison who had been doing time for beating up her cheating ex-husband. Sonyia stated that she had received a complete pardon after Shasa admitted her responsibility for the crime. It was very rewarding to witness a successful inmate in the community.

Segregation Visits

One sunny day when many inmates were outside in the yard trying to get a tan, I made a deliberate tour of segregation. I consciously made a strong effort to visit segregation once or twice per week. Periodically I visited segregation every day during the week. Sometimes I went during the day, other times at night, and occasionally over the weekend. The inmates in segregation were generally the most vulnerable and in need of human contact. In some instances, even a visit from the warden received some reaction. The human spirit is complex and not fully understood. Perhaps I identified with the inmates in segregation. Selfishly I was very aware that outside agencies and political watchdogs would be quick to respond if a major incident occurred in segregation. I was a strong advocate for staff to ensure that all visitors and staff signed the visitor's book. Some days there were twenty people who entered segregation and signed the segregation logbook.

When I visited the PC area, Mary Ann was cheerful and energetic. Mary Ann's taste in music changed greatly from when she was first admitted to the PFW. Her music interest changed from rock and roll to classical. Mary Ann always had classical music playing softly in her cell. She particularly enjoyed Glenn Gould's piano concertos and opera music, especially that sung by Joan Sutherland and Marie Callas. That day I asked her what was the beautiful music that she was listening to. She said it was music from *Madame Butterfly*.

I commented, "You are in a great mood. Is there something that I should know?"

Mary Ann looked at me with a smile on her face and said, "The teacher advised me today that in addition to regular pay she was paying me extra for being a tutor to three students in the PC area."

I replied, "Great! You deserve it, Mary Ann."

Her smile was infectious. She even laughed today. Mary Ann was gaining more and more confidence. She continued to work hard on her lesson plans for high school courses. She was a few months away from completing her Grade 13. Mary Ann received excellent school marks. They were all A's or B's. Her reading skill had greatly improved. She was reading more difficult books.

I also toured the other side of segregation. The inmates were all listening to some quiet music. Two Salvation Army staff were making their rounds from cell to cell. One inmate in segregation because of heavy drug usage asked me to come to her cell. Pauline was a young Native woman from a reserve in Northern Saskatchewan. She had received a letter from her father advising that he would be passing through Kingston in one week on his way to Montreal. He did not know that the Independent Chairperson (a judge) had sentenced Pauline to twenty days in segregation for intoxication and destroying some prison furniture.[9]

Pauline said in a quiet voice, "Warden, would you please give me permission to see my father next week? I haven't seen my family members for two years."

Inmates in segregation, for disciplinary reasons, did not receive visits, but in this case I approved Pauline's request for a closed visit. As previously stated, in my view visits are very important to help with an inmate's rehabilitation.

Pauline looked up and said, "Thank you, Warden." I observed small tears rolling down her face. Nothing more was said.

I passed by the Doukhobor cells and they were all lying down sleeping, since they had been up until three a.m. I exited segregation and continued my tour of the institution.

Christmas at the P4W

The months disappeared quickly. Soon it was Christmas 1982. A week before Christmas, Mary Ann gave me a portrait of myself that she had done. I was touched by her action. I generally don't

---

9   In the late seventies, the correctional service of Canada sometimes brought in citizens to conduct hearings in disciplinary court. Prior to this, wardens chaired the disciplinary court. The first independent chairpersons of the disciplinary court were all Liberal appointments. The appointments in the Kingston area were all lawyers. Later, in the eighties, when the Conservatives were in power, the chairpersons of the disciplinary courts were not reappointed, and Conservative appointees were hired.

buy Christmas gifts for inmates. This Christmas, however, I bought Mary Ann a little book entitled *The Little Prince*.

I lived close to the prison. Every Christmas morning, I made a special quick visit to the institution to wish inmates and staff a Merry Christmas. This was a difficult time for inmates. It is hard to walk by some inmates and wish them a Merry Christmas, knowing that I had turned down their Christmas pass one week before. Sometimes the community assessment for a three-day Christmas temporary pass was negative. Either a family member or child did not want the inmate to come home, or, in some cases, the inmate's behaviour in the institution did not warrant a pass. In other cases, the possibility of drinking excessive alcohol or using drugs in their own community was too great and posed too much risk. In some communities, the police would be adamantly opposed to any pass home, especially if the inmate had killed someone or caused serious bodily injuries.

I wish I could have approved all temporary passes at Christmas and New Year's, but it simply was not possible. For lifers, the Parole Board of Canada had to approve a temporary absence program. If the Parole Board did not approve, my hands were tied. In exceptional cases, the warden could recommend a special pass on humanitarian grounds.

Two days before Christmas, I was in the local city library and I read a small article in a Vancouver newspaper that got my attention. The article said that several buildings had been set on fire in the Kootenay Region of British Columbia. The RCMP strongly suspected that the Sons of Freedom Sect Doukhobors were responsible for this arson. I didn't realize it at the time, but this was the first sign that something was troubling the Doukhobors in the eastern interior of British Columbia.

Group Therapy in Protective Custody

In 1983, Mary Ann was the unofficial leader in the PC unit. One afternoon in early January when I was visiting the PC unit, I went to Mary Ann's cell. She was listening to music from one of Puccini's operas. Mary Ann made a comment about my social work background and interest in females who abused children.

During a previous discussion at her cell, Mary Ann was aware of my thesis on child abuse.

I remembered telling her that in 1971–72, I had counselled a female offender who had received life for killing a foster child in her care. The inmate was transferred to a mental hospital in Edmonton because she was depressed and refused to accept responsibility for the child's death. I saw this inmate weekly for one year and four months. During the second-last counselling session with her and her husband, Barbara finally admitted that she deliberately shook the baby foster child too hard and it broke the child's neck. It was difficult for her, but going over the events time and time again, she finally opened up. Her husband kissed her and said that was the first time in seven years that she had confessed to the crime.

Within six months, Barbara appeared before the National Parole Board. The chair of the National Parole Board and two other members went to the mental hospital and reviewed her application for full parole. The chief psychiatrist and I spoke in favour of her application. During the interview, Barbara admitted that she shook the baby hard and the baby's neck had broken. Barbara thanked me for helping her to come to terms with her actions and the child's death. She received full parole to return to her home and family. She was prohibited from having small children in her house. Four years later, I learned that Barbara had given birth to a little boy one year after receiving full parole.

Mary Ann asked me if I would conduct group therapy sessions for her and four other inmates. All five inmates had committed offences against children. I agreed to lead the group only if all five inmates participated. This was the only time as warden I ever conducted counselling sessions for inmates. (When I was a parole officer in 1973, I conducted a group session for eight male sex offenders.) Before I commenced the sessions with the PC inmates, I ran the idea past the inmates' classification officers. The classification officers all agreed with the sessions and commented that it would be a positive experience.

The first session started on Monday afternoon. I arranged that the assistant warden be informed that I would be asking the two correctional officers that sit in the PC area to move to the segregation side until the group sessions were over after ninety minutes. Once inside the PC area, I asked the two female correctional officers to position themselves behind the door in the segregation area. The guards could look periodically through the door window to ensure everything was okay. This would allow the inmates to speak more openly in a private area. I conducted the group sessions in the lower corridor hallway.

I conducted group sessions for five months. Initially, two of the five inmates refused to accept responsibility for their child's death. One of them broke down one afternoon and admitted that she was on drugs and did not mean to hurt her child. It was a major turning point in the group. The inmates did most of the talking. I let them talk. They got a lot of things off their chests.

The one inmate (Maggie) who refused to participate in the group sessions had no interest in changing her life. She hated life. She hated her family, her husband, and her children. Maggie was released one year later on Mandatory Supervision. Six months later, she was killed during a robbery attempt in a small bar in Montreal. Maggie shot at a bartender who had a gun under the bar. He fired one shot as she was leaving the bar and hit her in the neck.

Mary Ann was finding it very hard being locked up in the small PC area. She had almost finished her high school courses, including Grade 13, and was looking into starting some university correspondence courses. She was doing her best to stay focused, but the period of dead time rattled her. She smoked a lot and drank lots of coffee.

Irene's Story

Wardens and other administrators who are responsible for female inmates are sometimes faced with difficult decisions to save an inmate from harm or reach an inmate who is very depressed and in despair. I recall an incident in 1979 that required an extraordinary solution to solve the problem.

There was a small, wiry, middle-aged woman named Irene who was confined in segregation because of bizarre, disruptive behaviour. Irene was a fifty-three-year-old white ex-soldier who had a severe alcoholic problem. She was admitted to the PFW in 1977 for attempted murder. Irene stabbed a male suitor who refused to do something she wanted done. Irene was sentenced to six years. For two years, Irene's behaviour was non-problematic. But in the spring of 1979, Irene had to be removed from the population and placed in segregation. She was acting crazy and disrupting the range where she resided. She would yell in her cell at the top of her voice late at night. Some of the negative things she screamed out were very disturbing. Irene would throw her clothes and personal effects out of her cell onto the corridor floor. Inmates complained that her antics kept the entire range up at night. It was necessary to place her in segregation.

Irene's behaviour got worse in segregation. She would climb the cell bars like a monkey and hang in awkward positions looking down at people walking by in the range. She suffered from extreme hallucinations and bad dreams. Her previous alcoholic indulgences during her adult years had had an adverse effect on her health.

Irene was seen by the institutional physician, nurses, chaplain, psychologist, psychiatrist, classification officer, and senior staff. I don't think there was any professional staff member who did not interview Irene or try to help solve her problems. She became very paranoid and talked to herself. After eight weeks in segregation, her behaviour became severe. She stopped eating. Between the nursing staff and the food steward officer, everything was done to help her gain some weight. The Chief of Health Care had Irene checked over by the institutional physician and the psychiatrist. The psychiatrist prescribed some medications for her depression, but they did not help. Irene's flashbacks and bad dreams were getting worse. The doctor was at a loss. He suggested we find out what food Irene loved to eat and bring it to her. It worked for one week; then she stopped eating altogether. The doctor reported that Irene had lost twenty-five pounds, dropping from 110 pounds to 85 pounds.

A special meeting was called including myself, the Chief of Health Care, AW Security, and the doctor. We were desperate. Someone suggested that we get her a kitten. We arranged for a kitten to be placed in her cell. She neglected the kitten.

The doctor was concerned that Irene might have organ failure if she continued to refuse food. She did drink water and some tea. After six days of not eating, force feeding by tube was discussed. Someone said it was not medically ethical.

I remember the head nurse made a suggestion that flabbergasted the group. If Irene refused food for three more days, she could become very ill and would have to be placed in the prison health care centre. The nurse said she remembered an alcoholic patient who would not eat, so family members gave the patient some dark stout. After three days, the patient began to improve. The AW Security said no beer or other alcohol was allowed in the prison.

We were at a stalemate. What could we do? Finally a nurse said, "Let's get some stout and smuggle it into the prison. It can be brought into the hospital and used for medicinal purposes." After considerable discussion, there was agreement. A plan was put in motion. The institutional driver would pick up the beer and carry it in a large cloth bag past the two correctional officers that were stationed at the main front control post.

When the time came, one curious guard asked the driver, "Tom, what is in the bag?"

The driver replied, "Some medical supplies for the hospital." The beer was delivered to the hospital and kept in the locked room where narcotics were stored.

It was arranged that Irene would be called up to the hospital after inmate medication parade was completed. The first time Irene was called to the hospital was priceless. A guard went to her cell and said, "Irene, get dressed. You are called to the hospital for some medicine." Irene was escorted to the hospital and asked to sit on a chair and wait until she was called. The Chief of Health Care called Irene into the examination room and asked her to sit on a small table. Irene was very weak and could hardly speak. The nurse said to Irene in a loud voice, "I hear you are not eating and you have no appetite."

Irene stared at the nurse in bewilderment. She did not speak. The nurse turned around and said, "Irene, I am going to give you something to help you regain your appetite."

Irene looked at the drink before her. She sniffed the beer but did not take a drink. Irene was a bit paranoid at times. She did not trust the nurse. The nurse proceeded to work on her paperwork. After twenty-two minutes, Irene took a small sip of the beer. Her brain started to work. It sparked a reaction. It jump-started her memory. She took another sip, and then another. Yes! She remembered the good taste of beer. Within two minutes, the large beer glass was empty. Irene looked puzzled. I suspect she was wondering what the nurses were doing to her. Were they trying to poison her? Irene had not drunk alcohol in three years.

Irene was returned to her cell in segregation. She was called back to the hospital at 6:30 p.m. The nurse offered Irene another glass of stout. This time Irene finished the beer in three large gulps. Irene left the hospital with a little smile or smirk on her face. For three successive days, Irene drank two beers, one in the morning and one in the early evening. By the end of the third day, Irene finished the beer in one large gulp. She wanted a second beer.

Irene went back to segregation feeling good. A special meal—her favourite, a small steak with mashed potatoes and gravy—was brought to her. Irene slowly ate the entire meal.

Irene had two beers a day for six more days. She started eating regularly. By the end of day seven, Irene was escorted to the hospital. There was no more beer for her. The nurse gave Irene a mild sedative to help relax her and help her sleep. The next day, Irene saw the psychologist, who helped her understand her problems. Irene was free of nightmares and bad dreams. It took three weeks before Irene was eating and sleeping normally. Irene was returned to her cell on the range. In four months, Irene was released to a halfway house. I should comment that there were no entries in Irene's medical file that said she received beer in the hospital. It was against prison regulations to bring alcohol into the prison.

Looking back, this was a risky move. Each time Irene was brought to the nursing station to receive a beer, the inmate cleaner, who had a drinking problem, was released to her living area. It was important that no inmates and minimal staff be aware of this plan to help Irene regain her strength. We were concerned that inmates would try to steal the beer if they knew it was in the hospital; or they might want the same treatment that Irene received. It was a bold, imaginative decision to allow beer into the institution just this once. In this case, it worked miracles. I don't remember alcohol ever being brought into the prison again.

3

The Doukhobors — An Unhealthy Situation

As the months passed, I became increasingly concerned about the Doukhobor inmates in segregation. As a group, they were not eating enough food to sustain life. I contacted a local Ukrainian Catholic church and spoke to a church leader and asked for his help. He indicated that the church ladies made *holubtsi* (cabbage rolls), borscht (Russian beet soup), and other foods that Russian and Ukrainian people eat. I was given the name of a lady church parishioner who agreed to cook a large batch of Ukrainian–Russian foods. I brought in the food in warming trays and delivered it the Doukhobor inmates. It was my luck that Marta B. and Molly A. were attending a medical clinic in the afternoon. A correctional officer and I dished out the warm food to each Doukhobor inmate. To my surprise, the five inmates ate the large meal.

Two hours later, the two Doukhobor leaders entered the segregation area. We prepared the warm food for them. They did not take it, so we put it in their cells. Later that day, I was told that the two leaders had finished off the borscht but did not eat the other solid foods. The next week, I returned with the same amount of food while the two Doukhobor leaders were at the dentist. The five inmates ate the food. When the two Doukhobor inmate leaders returned, they would not eat any food. The next week, I returned with more food. This time no Doukhobor inmate would eat any of the prepared food. We were back to square one.

During the next four weeks, the health of the Doukhobor inmates improved because of the wonderful intervention of a Roman Catholic nun. At the time, the prison had an old Roman Catholic priest named Father Dion as the prison chaplain. Father Dion offered mass weekly on Saturday and conducted confessions as well. Father Dion spoke with a strong French accent.

Few inmates spent time on Saturday with Father Dion. After one and half hours he exited the prison.

In actual truth, the real asset in the chaplain department was a Roman Catholic nun named Monica. Although she was not the formal chaplain, it is safe to say that she was respected by both the inmates and staff. She spent many hours in the prison, talking to and counselling inmates. Sister Monica cared deeply for the inmates and was always available night and day for them. On numerous occasions, Sister Monica escorted inmates into the community and completed family visits.

One day, Sister Monica approached me in the chapel and said, "I have a plan to get the Doukhobor inmates to eat." She explained that prayer would help these inmates. Sister Monica asked to have all the interested Doukhobor inmates attend the chapel. She estimated that five out of the seven would attend the chapel together. I was out of options. I agreed that Sunday morning I would have staff escort the interested Doukhobor inmates to the chapel to pray. The chapel was searched, and candles and matches were locked up. The chapel was free for a group meeting.

On Monday morning, Sister Monica was surprised that all seven Doukhobor inmates had arrived in the chapel. Sister had arranged for recorded Russian music and had several prayers translated into English. In addition, she had borscht and bread available. The women ate the soup, with the bread, and sang Russian songs. They all prayed together. Sister Monica stated that it was truly an uplifting experience.

Sister arranged the same program for four weeks in duration. The format each week was the same. It was amazing what occurred in the chapel. Within two weeks, the inmates had gained three pounds.

After completing the fourth week, the Doukhobor inmates went back to refusing most food. This time, the two leaders were not interested in taking meals. Everything changed after Marta B. was allowed a telephone call to her husband. Later we heard that her daughter and granddaughter had been arrested and sent to jail. Marta B. and Molly A. started their fast again. Sister Monica's intervention had helped for a short time but it, too, could not convince the Doukhobors to eat.

One afternoon the following week, my secretary knocked on my door and said that a Salvation Army officer named Jenkins would like to have a few words with me. The officer and I had a good relationship. She explained that the youngest of the Doukhobor women, Mary, who was being released in three weeks, had confided in her. She related that Marta B. and Molly A. were determined to starve themselves to death in protest against the government for persecuting their people and putting them in prison. Mary was genuinely concerned. She further explained that somehow the Sons of Freedom Doukhobor Sect in the Kootenay Region of British Columbia were planning something big. Mary did not want to spill the beans. Officer Jenkins stressed that it would be problematic if either woman starved herself to death in prison. Officer Jenkins said that she would advise me if she received additional information.

Later that day, I called a meeting with the Assistant Warden Security and the Chief of Health Care, Mrs. Thomas. She was a very intelligent woman in her late thirties. She was a perfectionist who strived to improve the health care for the inmates. Mrs. Thomas handled her stress by smoking. She had been at the prison for ten years. She was promoted to head nurse in 1977. I had a lot of confidence in her abilities and her understanding of the important issues in running a prison. She fought very hard to obtain resources for the health care centre. I informed them of my conversation with Officer Jenkins. I directed Mrs. Thomas to have her nurses monitor the two Doukhobor leaders very closely. During their regular visits to segregation, the nurses were going to check the vital signs of the two leaders. The head nurse suggested that we obtain some special tea that had some nutrients. The two Doukhobor leaders continued to drink tea and water. The two leaders were escorted to the health care centre weekly to be checked by the institutional physician and weighed. Everything was being done to monitor the Doukhobors' situation and improve their health.

Hostile Acts towards Staff

During the years I was in management, from 1975 until almost 1988, I had to deal with a number of incidents where inmates physically assaulted staff. People in the community asked me many times if I was scared to work in a maximum-security female prison. Over the years, staff have received different injuries, including physical and mental assaults. Some staff were punched, kicked, slapped, and hit with furniture and other items. In certain cases, some staff members were assaulted by several inmates, usually high under the influence of brew or drugs.

I remember one day in 1981 when two female correctional officers tried to remove two inmates to segregation. The two inmates grabbed several chairs and broke off the legs. High on drugs, the two inmates attacked the officers. One officer was badly beaten around the face. In addition, she sustained injuries to her shoulder, arms, and legs. This officer was off work for five months. The other officer at the scene had two teeth knocked out and lost part of her hair from her scalp. However, incidents of violence against staff were generally rare. Violent incidents against staff where injuries occurred usually happened when trying to calm down intoxicated inmates, removing them from the population to segregation, or in the act of charging a given inmate.

Sometimes aggressive female inmates who are boisterous and possess intimidating manners create a difficult atmosphere for new employees. I recall one day in 1982. A new female clerk started work in the case management area. The inmates passed the classification area on their way to the school. The young, attractive, twenty-four-year-old employee was not ready for what she experienced. She was swarmed by a number of loud-mouthed lesbian inmates who were like bees after honey. After twenty-five minutes of continuous attention and inappropriate comments, the young clerk grabbed her coat and ran out of institution. When she reached the front door, she told the correctional officer manning the control post that she could not work in this environment and was not coming back. Over the years, I had several new employees quit their jobs within several weeks. They realized it was a difficult work environment and not suited for them.

As a young warden, I experienced several serious situations that necessitated bringing in the Emergency Response Team from Kingston Penitentiary. One evening in 1983, I received a telephone call at home around eight-thirty p.m. from the Duty

"A" Block in the Prison for Women. (Courtesy Corrections Service Canada Museum

Correctional Supervisor in charge of the prison that night. The supervisor reported that we had a hostage situation. A violent thirty-three-year-old Native inmate named Mandy, who was from Manitoba, had taken a new, young, and attractive correctional officer hostage by putting a shiv (homemade knife) at her throat and forcing her into her cell.

Mandy was a true maximum-security inmate, serving a life sentence for murder. Previously, she had served a ten-year sentence for manslaughter. She had killed a man during a heavy drinking party. Mandy was unpredictable. She had been in the prison since 1975, and there was little chance she would be released on parole for many years. She posed too much risk for the community. Mandy had serious substance abuse problems coupled with violent emotional outbursts. She was an aggressive lesbian who had had several partners over the years. No one in the institution had been aware that she fancied the new correctional officer.

I told the correctional supervisor I would be in shortly. I telephoned the Duty Correctional Supervisor at Kingston Penitentiary and asked him to call in the Emergency Response Team because we had a hostage situation. I asked the correctional supervisor at the Prison for Women to telephone the AW Security and tell her she was required at the prison. I arrived at the institution in five minutes. The crisis management model was implemented. A number of staff were brought in to help manage the crisis. I contacted the Deputy Commissioner of Ontario and advised him of the hostage situation. Officer Brown's husband was contacted and briefed on the ongoing situation.

The crisis management centre was in my office area. After receiving a briefing from the Duty Correctional Supervisor, I assumed control of the emergency incident. A second security supervisor was deployed to the "A" range post, where several correctional officers were observing the incident. I reviewed the matter with my senior staff and selected Sister Monica to be the hostage negotiator, because she had excellent rapport with the Native inmates; they trusted her.

It was quiet on "A" range. All the inmates returned to their cells. Inmates in other living units were locked in their cells. Within forty-five minutes, eight members of the Emergency Response Team from Kingston Penitentiary arrived at the prison. This was a team of specially trained correctional officers who were prepared to manage any serious situation. The team looked like something out of a *Star Wars* movie. They wore black fatigue clothing. They had large helmets with Plexiglas covering their eyes and faces. They had large chest protectors, black gloves, and knee and elbow pads. The team used large shields for protection and batons as weapons. Each officer carried mace and pepper spray. The team also had lethal weapons like rifles and shotguns, to be used if required. The team when activated would march in unison to a loud cadence of batons and shields making stressful, intimidating sounds. I briefed the team leader and asked him to get his team dressed and report upstairs to the landing outside "B" range.

The team leader carried a walkie-talkie and was prepared to respond when directed by the warden. Within seven minutes, the team was dressed.

All was still quiet on the "A" range. Mandy's cell was the fourteenth cell from the range barrier—about seventy feet from the barrier. The correctional officer opened the barrier and Sister Monica proceeded down the range. Monica yelled out, "Mandy, this is Monica. Is everything okay?"

Mandy yelled back, "Don't come any closer. I will hurt the bitch if you come closer." Mandy seemed agitated.

Monica spoke up, "Is Officer Brown okay?"

A few seconds went by before Officer Brown shouted, "I am okay."

Mandy yelled that she needed some pop and cigarettes. Monica said, "Give me a few minutes." Monica returned and was instructed by Mandy to place the pop and cigarettes outside the cell. Monica did as requested. The staff at the barrier observed Mandy using a large broom to drag the items into her cell.

The tension at the scene was growing. Officers were concerned about the fate of one of their own. After fifteen minutes, Monica entered the range. "Mandy, it is Monica. I am on the range. What are your concerns at this time?"

After a few minutes, Mandy yelled out, "I am concerned about my mother. I received word that she is dying."

Monica replied, "Please let Officer Brown go and we will arrange for you to call your father."

Mandy yelled for Monica to get back. Silence prevailed. Twenty-five minutes passed and nothing. It was 9:45 p.m., and the tension was mounting. Finally, Mandy yelled at Monica, "If I let Officer Brown go, can I telephone my father tonight?"

Monica checked with me via phone and shouted out, "It will be arranged."

Mandy said, "Okay."

After five minutes, Officer Brown was released. She was crying and her clothes were in disarray. Monica yelled for Mandy to throw out her knife. A small sharp knife with black tape wrapped around its handle was thrown out of the cell onto the range floor. The Emergency Response Team members entered the range and secured the inmate. Mandy's cell was searched. Mandy was handcuffed and taken to segregation. Her cell was secured as a crime scene. Later, she was given a telephone call to her father.

Activity Building, 1982.
(Courtesy Corrections
Service Canada Museum)

Officer Brown was taken to the health care centre and examined by a doctor. She was comforted by the nursing staff and the AW Security. The ambulance was released from the institution. The city police were called and advised of the incident. A debriefing session was conducted with staff and the Emergency Response Team personnel. The psychologist helped with the stress debriefing. A lot of reports were completed.

After an interview with the doctor, Officer Brown went to the local hospital with her husband and a female correctional officer who was close to her. Later, the police went to the hospital and interviewed Officer Brown, then returned to the institution and interviewed staff. I was happy that everything worked out okay. I thanked the staff for a good job. I approached Sister Monica and thanked her for her participation.

Officer Brown had a difficult time adjusting to her ordeal. She experienced some emotional issues and post-traumatic stress. She never returned to the Prison for Women. After one year, she was transferred to a male prison. She worked two months and then decided to quit the service. Mandy was charged and found guilty of forceful confinement and given additional years on her life sentence. Although it never came out in court, it is quite possible that Officer Brown was sexually assaulted in the cell by the inmate.

The writer has known several employees who were taken hostage in a prison environment. In each case, the event has changed the individual and affected his/her view of the world. As for myself, I experienced two hostage events and must admit each event has helped to diminish and remove my trusting nature towards people.

I used the Emergency Response Team from Kingston Penitentiary one other time during my tenure as warden. In 1984, three large and aggressive inmates were extremely intoxicated on "A" range. These three inmates were very dangerous and had a long history of violence. They were destroying government property and threatening the staff. I was called at home at 10:30 p.m. I arrived at the institution within ten minutes. The Duty Correctional Supervisor informed me that three or four inmates were destroying several cells on "A" range and were threatening the staff. One correctional officer was lucky to have escaped their grasp. She had locked the cell range just in time as the inmates began throwing heavy articles at her.

The inmates removed large furniture items from their cells and built a barricade across the corridor landing. Correctional officers were threatened if they entered the range. The duty correctional officer tried to convince the inmates to drop their weapons and return to their cells. The rest of the range inmates were locked in their cells. When I witnessed the mental condition of the inmates, plus the weapons they had in their hands, including a razor blade knife, steel pipes, and wooden table legs, I knew it would be necessary to call in the Emergency Response Team. The three inmates had smashed twenty windows on the range and were trying to start a small fire.

The team was called at 10:45 p.m. I contacted the Duty Correctional Supervisor at KP and asked for his assistance. I said we had an incident where three or four intoxicated inmates were destroying the range and threatening the staff. The team arrived at the prison at 11:45 p.m. and got dressed. I briefed the team leader and said I would give the inmates one more opportunity to retreat to their cells.

I walked up the stairs at the barrier to "A" range. I told the inmates, "You have three minutes to put down your weapons and enter your cells."

The inmates laughed and said, in a violent manner, "What are you going to do? Come and get us." They threw small bottles with oil that were on fire.

I directed the inmates three times to desist and return to their cells. They became more violent and uncooperative. I told them the Emergency Response Team would enter the range if they did not return to their cells. I directed the team to enter the range. The door opened, and the loud noise of the eight-member team's banging on their shields with their batons caused considerable panic and alarm as they marched in cadence closer and closer to the three inmates. A fourth intoxicated inmate passed out in her cell.

The team leader told his men to pull out their mace and pepper spray. The inmates were so intoxicated the presence of the team meant nothing. After they had received a considerable amount of mace and a small amount of pepper spray, they yelled, "Come and get us, you fucking pigs!" The team was taken by surprise when the three inmates attacked them. It was total confusion. Inmates who were locked in their cells and had sympathy for the three attackers threw articles through their bars and hit some of the team members as they advanced.

The clash between the three inmates and the nine-member team lasted about seven minutes before the three inmates were subdued. The whole event resembled a large bowling ball smashing into tenpins—bodies with legs and arms landing all over the place. One team member received a knife wound, while another had his leg hit hard with a metal bar. The three inmates were handcuffed and taken to segregation. Staff removed the barricade and locked up the three inmates' cells. I conducted a staff debriefing with the Emergency Response Team and staff before the involved staff exited the building and were relieved.

I was really appreciative of the Emergency Response Team's involvement. In previous years, many staff would have been used to end a disturbance, and most likely this could have resulted in a number of staff's being injured. The Emergency Response Team was used extensively in larger male prisons. Its role became a common occurrence when serious problems arose in the prisons.

Sometimes verbal attacks and accusations left deep emotional scars on staff if they were unjustly targeted. I vividly remember a well-respected male shop instructor named Raymond who was accused in 1983 of sexually inappropriate actions against an inmate named Jane, who had limited education. Jane accused the male instructor of making a sexual pass towards her. I had a senior staff member conduct an investigation. After all the information and interview notes were reviewed, it was clear that Jane had attempted to discredit the male instructor because he fired her lesbian girlfriend for stealing shop materials. Raymond was cleared on all charges.

Industrial sewing room, 1985.
(Courtesy Corrections Service Canada Museum)

Six months later, Jane reported that Raymond had made another inappropriate sexual approach. In order to gain some impartiality, I asked the chair of the Citizen Advisory Committee (CAC) to investigate Jane's charge. The CAC was created in the late seventies. Each institution and parole office in Federal

Corrections was directed by the Commissioner of Corrections to have a group of volunteers that met monthly with the administration and inmates to review and ameliorate potential and real problems in the institution and with parole events.

After two weeks, the CAC chair submitted her report. Raymond was very nervous, because if the charge were proven, his employment in corrections would be at risk. The chair of the CAC reported that Jane was vindictive and wanted to get Raymond fired. The chair of the inmate committee commented that the investigation was fair. She told me a friend of Jane's openly admitted that the charge was untrue and that she had it in for Raymond. I told Raymond the results of the investigation. He was found not guilty. He broke down and wept. Raymond was a hard-working instructor who loved his job and was happy in his married life. This charge against Raymond had a severe impact on his health. One year later, he was off work for stress-related leave. Raymond returned two months later and proved to be one of the best shop instructors in the prison.

In many ways, serving time in a prison is like a giant bingo machine throwing up many balls with letters and numbers on them. Inmates are personally assigned a number on a ball. The balls bounce around, never knowing when they will be called. There are many balls in the air at any given time. Sometimes a number is called that brings an element of closure. As previously stated, some staff cross the line and quietly become involved with an inmate—with tragic consequences.

During the last few years of the 1970s, one correctional officer was secretly involved with an inmate named Gerry who had limited intelligence and possessed great physical strength. Gerry was easy prey for a mature and cunning woman. Although the senior staff had their suspicions, there was insufficient evidence to intervene. In early 1980, Gerry served her sentence and was released to the community. Several months later, Gerry was charged with the murder of a correctional officer. The correctional officer had invited Gerry to live with her in her apartment. One night, Gerry came home and noticed through a window that her correctional officer girlfriend was in bed having sex with a black man. She waited until the black man left the house. Gerry entered the house and in rage she strangled the correctional officer to death. Given her limited intelligence and the fact that she was a controlled person, the court reduced her charge from murder to manslaughter. She was sentenced to ten years and returned to the Prison for Women. Gerry served eight more years and was released again to the community. She died from a brain tumour less than one year later.

Inmate Tutoring

Given the many balls in the air that required a lot of my attention, I did not spend as much time with Mary Ann during the following six months as I would have liked. In late 1983, Mary Ann's education reached a new level. She had finished her high school courses and was doing exceptionally well with her college correspondence courses. One day I heard the schoolteacher tell Mary Ann's classification officer that she was ready for college. Since Mary Ann was not eligible for day parole for another year, I suggested that Mary Ann continue to be a tutor for two Native inmates in protective custody. Mary Ann excelled in math, English, and drawing. She convinced two inmates in protective custody to take high school courses. Mary Ann agreed to be their mentor. She did everything she could to help the two students with their studies.

One of the two students was a twenty-two-year-old Native girl from Saskatchewan. She had had a serious problem with school, especially math. The other student was from New Brunswick. She was really slow and had a difficult time with junior high school courses. One day I toured the segregation range. I stopped in at the PC unit first. I found Mary Ann playing a reading game with her two students. I could tell she was immersed in her role as a tutor.

Doukhobors' Fasting; Intervention

One of the balls I was concentrating on during the last week of 1983 was the eating habits of the Doukhobor inmates. The majority of them would eat some amounts of food periodically, but not the two ringleaders. Marta B. and Molly A. were carrying their fasting to a new level. Molly A. fasted and became weaker. She would drink tea and water. Her weight dropped from 135 pounds to ninety-eight pounds. After several weeks of strict fasting, Molly was taken to the Health Care Centre to see the institutional doctor. The doctor told her that if she continued to fast, she could expect kidney problems, and as well other organs in her body would be stressed. The doctor emphasized that if she got too weak, she would not be in a position to receive visits. Also, if she continued fasting, she would eventually have to be transferred to a community hospital once she became semi-conscious and near death. This reality posed by the doctor seemed to reach the inmate.

One of the Salvation Army representatives expressed concern about the two ladies. I suspect one of the officers telephoned Molly's husband and revealed her serious condition.

A few days later, I received a telephone call from Molly's husband from British Columbia. He asked me if his wife was really ill. I said that if she continued with her fast, she could be transferred to a community hospital that deals with patients that are near death. The husband asked if he could have a long visit with his wife if he came to the institution. He wanted to tell her that she was going to be a grandmother the following month. Her daughter and future baby, as well as himself, all wanted her to stay alive. He said that he would try to convince his wife to give up her fast. I approved a special long visit for Saturday morning, two days from then.

On Saturday morning, Molly had a lengthy visit with her husband in the visiting room. There were no other inmates in the room. He brought her a small box of tin cans full of Doukhobor foods, which was left for my attention.

On Monday morning, I gave the food to the chief food steward. He opened one can and inspected the food. He agreed to heat up the food from two cans and arranged for a female food steward officer to take it to the two ringleaders. To my great surprise and that of the other concerned staff, Molly ate the prepared Doukhobor food. On the other hand, Marta B. continued with her fast. Molly received a can of hot Doukhobor food each day and ate the food. Within one week, she had gained two pounds. Molly seemed genuinely interested in returning home to be with her family.

When Molly's husband returned home, he gave a comprehensive briefing to Marta's husband and other family members. There was real concern that Marta would die in prison. Several weeks passed, and Marta's condition became critical. A special meeting was held between myself, the Chief of Health Care, and the AW Security. The issue of force-feeding was discussed. The health care representatives stated that it was not approved or sanctioned to force-feed an inmate patient by placing feeding tubes into her body. The doctor remarked that unless Marta ate food or drank more liquids, she would have to be placed in a community hospital in two or three weeks or less.

Something extraordinary happened in the Kootenays within the next ten days. A number of Doukhobor supporters in the interior (Creston Valley) of British Columbia around Krestova started a number of fires, burning small buildings using gasoline and matches. Each day the number of fires increased. Naked Doukhobor men and women stood at the fire sites and protested the incarceration of Marta in Kingston. After three days of small buildings being destroyed by fire and naked Doukhobors protesting, the superintendent of the Royal Canadian Mounted Police responsible for the Kootenay Region of British Columbia knew he had a serious problem on his hands.

An Irish staff sergeant named O'Brien of the RCMP detachment in Nelson, British Columbia, telephoned me and introduced himself. He reported that he had done an investigation twenty years ago with my boss. O'Brien, who had a strong Irish accent, seemed like he was a man on a fishing expedition. He said, "I wonder, Warden, can you help me?"

I responded, "It all depends. What is on your mind?"

He responded, "We have a serious situation in the Kootenay Region that seems to be escalating." He asked me straight out, "I understand that you have several Doukhobors in segregation and that some of them are quite ill. Do you have a Marta B. in segregation?"

I replied, "Affirmative."

"Is she very ill?"

I spoke clearly and said that she was ill because of her fast. I told O'Brien that Marta was the only committed Doukhobor determined to fast to the death. I emphasized that there was a real possibility that Marta could die in prison. The staff sergeant was extremely concerned and stressed that the entire region could go up in smoke if she became a martyr and died in prison. He explained that she had a lot of fanatical Doukhobor sympathizers in the Creston Valley. O'Brien suggested that we keep in touch and that it would be prudent to inform our respective bosses.

I contacted the Deputy Commissioner for Ontario within two days after he returned from holidays and briefed him of the situation regarding the Doukhobors. My boss said that he would advise the Commissioner of Corrections and make sure the Solicitor General of Canada was up to speed on the matter.

First thing on Monday morning, I contacted the Chief of Health Care and received a current medical report on inmate Marta B. Mrs. Thomas told me that Marta was getting worse and had lost another five pounds. I asked Mrs. Thomas to arrange for a meeting in the Health Care Centre with the doctor and herself, the AW Inmate Programs, and the AW Security for 10:00 a.m. that day.

At the meeting, I asked the doctor how long before inmate Marta would have to be admitted to an outside hospital and how long before her final days. The doctor was reluctant to pinpoint a time, but she could last one or two weeks or less if we gave her nutrient-base tea. The issue of force-feeding was resurrected. It died a quiet death. The AW Inmate Programs had an idea that got the group's attention. If inmate Marta were strong and alert enough, we could get her to apply for parole with exception. Given her frail medical condition, the AW said there might be another way. In exceptional cases we could get her husband to apply for a humanitarian parole and rush it through quickly to Ottawa. I said I would call Marta's husband today and see if he would come right away. The nursing staff were directed to monitor Marta every two hours.

I telephoned Marta's husband, and by chance he was at home. I told him his wife was very ill and needed to eat, or she would fall into a coma and die. I explained that she was not mentally alert enough to apply for a parole with exception, but if he signed the application, we could do our best to get Marta home to her own community. I told him, "If you travel tomorrow, I will stay in the institution until you arrive."

There was brief silence. Mr. B. asked what the chance was that she could get it. I said, "The doctor, psychiatrist, the health care staff, her classification officer, and the senior staff all will support this application." It was her best chance to get out of the Prison for Women and return home.

At 7:30 p.m., Mr. B. arrived at the institution and signed the application. His wife was too weak to come to the Health Care Centre, so the AW Security and I escorted him down the hallway to the back door of segregation. He had a thirty-minute visit with his wife at the entrance landing outside segregation. We stood about ten feet away to ensure no matches or contraband were passed between husband and wife. I am not sure Marta realized what was happening. Mr. B. thanked me for the visit and said he would stay in Kingston until a decision was reached about his wife. I contacted Marta's experienced classification officer and asked him how things were going with respect to the documentation and the final report. He told me he would complete the report that evening, and in the morning we could have the driver take the package to Ottawa.

The next morning, before nine a.m., I received a telephone call directly from the Solicitor General for Canada. I had met him several times during the past two years in Ottawa while attending a maximum security warden's conference. The Solicitor General reported that he was getting heat from the RCMP in British Columbia, and of course questions from members of the NDP in the House of Commons. He asked for an update, since he was sure this would be a very serious matter that needed to be resolved quickly. I told him that we were sending an application package that day to the National Parole Board requesting a humanitarian parole for this very ill inmate. He was completely briefed on Doukhobor problems in the Kootenay Region of British Columbia.

The driver delivered the Parole with Exception package to the National Parole Board office in Ottawa at twelve noon. The classification officer had contacted senior staff at the National

Parole Board to advise them that the application for humanitarian parole was on the way to them. The week before, he had discussed this matter with an experienced case management official.

About three p.m., I received a call from the National Parole Board. The management official said that given the urgency of this application, they would try to obtain a decision within one week. I told them that the inmate could be dead by that time. He explained that all the Parole Board members were at a conference in Eastern Canada.

At three-thirty p.m., I telephoned the Solicitor General's chief of staff and explained that the exceptional parole decision could take a week. The executive assistant was aware of this matter and of the urgency to get things moving. He said he would meet the Solicitor General in thirty minutes and advise me of what decision would be made.

At 4:01 p.m., I received a telephone call from the executive assistant. He told me the complete package was being taken to executive council of cabinet this night and with luck, Mrs. B. would receive an executive clemency decision. He asked me to work on plans to transport the inmate within the next few days.

After receiving this telephone call, I asked the Chief of Health Care and the AW Security to start making arrangements to fly Marta home to the interior of British Columbia. I stayed late in the office that night. I ordered pizza for the four staff working on this matter.

Mrs. Thomas loved responsibility. At six p.m., she walked into my office and said, "If a decision comes tonight, I have arranged for a plane to fly from Kingston to Vancouver tomorrow at 11:00 a.m. The plane will fly to a small airport in British Columbia's interior, where medical staff and her family will be waiting for her." Mrs. Thomas further commented, "It won't be cheap." She was always concerned about her budget. She told me that the doctor, herself as a nurse, and one correctional officer would be escorting inmate Marta to British Columbia. I called the three staff to join me for some pizza and soda pops.

At nine p.m., I received a telephone call from the executive assistant. He advised that Mrs. B. had been granted a release under executive clemency. I thanked him for the help. Within half an hour, I received a fax confirming Marta's release. I contacted the husband, who was overjoyed. He was taking a train that night and would be flying to Calgary at seven a.m. and then to Nelson, British Columbia. He expressed his appreciation for all the work that had been done to get this decision approved.

When I got home at eleven-thirty p.m., I poured myself a good stiff rye drink. My wife asked me, "How was your day?"

I said, "Routine."

The next day, inmate Marta B. was sedated and placed on a hospital stretcher. The doctor, the Chief of Health Care, and an experienced correctional officer boarded a jet in Kingston at 11:00 a.m. and headed west. Their trip was uneventful. I telephoned Staff Sergeant O'Brien and informed him that inmate Marta B. was being transported by plane that day and would be in his area late this afternoon. O'Brien thanked me and said, "I owe you a large Guinness!"

After Marta B. left, the Doukhobor inmates ate their meals and regained their weight. Within ten months, six of the remaining Doukhobor inmates were released from prison and returned to British Columbia.

The Sons of Freedom Doukhobor inmates in the Creston Valley discontinued their arson activities after Marta B. returned. I remember the day that Molly was released from the Prison for Women. She thanked me for allowing her husband to have a special visit with her. She also expressed her appreciation for arranging for Marta to be returned to her community. Before she left the building, I overheard Molly tell a matron that she would never be back. She was going home to care for a new granddaughter. Molly A. was the last Doukhobor inmate to leave the prison

About five years later, I read in a Vancouver paper that Marta B. was arrested again for participating in another arson attack in the Creston Valley. This time, she received a short provincial sentence of eighteen months. After Molly left the prison, we never had another Doukhobor inmate in the Prison for Women.

In the early sixties, hundreds of Sons of Freedom Doukhobors marched from the Creston Valley near Krestova to the maximum security Agassiz prison, where ninety to one hundred

Doukhobor males were incarcerated in a special fireproof prison wing after the mass burnings and bombing of 1961 and 1962. The large group that marched to Agassiz prison was comprised mostly of women and children. They set up a camp outside the gates of the prison. In 1963, this group joined forces with many hundreds of Doukhobors and continued to camp in front of the prison in support of their husbands, fathers, uncles, and brothers in jail.[10]

In 1962, the Sons of Freedom Doukhobors had lost their rights to educate their children at home. The government of British Columbia decreed that all young children had to be educated in the public school system. At the time, I was a Grade 12 student in a high school not far from the encampment. I recall the students in my history class discussing the merits of their cause. In my opinion, this was the most important factor that exposed the Doukhobor children to the outside world and influenced them in their future endeavours. As they grew up and became educated, the young Doukhobor children refused to participate and become terrorists and arsonists like their mothers, fathers, uncles, aunts, grandmothers, and grandfathers. They became assimilated into British Columbia's mosaic and took their place in society. It was the end of an era.

Prison Entertainment

During the last quarter of 1983, I arranged for a professional performer to visit the institution and entertain the population. One night in early November, I took my wife to a local night club. We were entertained by a very energetic and impressive Elvis Presley impersonator. This young man was a very good singer and had Elvis Presley's mannerisms down pat. Following his first set break, I approached the singer and introduced myself. I asked him if he and his band had ever played in a prison. I revealed that I was the warden of the Prison for Women. I told the singer that I and scores of females in prison were Elvis fans. The singer, who later became a big hit in Los Vegas, agreed to entertain the inmates the next day.

---

10   Simma Holt, *Terror in the Name of God*, 9.

The next day was Friday. Early in the morning at a briefing meeting, I asked the Chief of Social Development to set up the gymnasium for a concert at three p.m. The AW Security agreed to look after the security arrangements for the band. I interviewed the chairperson of the Inmate Committee and told her that I had arranged for an Elvis Presley impersonator and his band to entertain the population. The chairperson was a big Elvis Presley fan. She made sure every inmate and staff in the prison was aware of the concert.

I must admit that I didn't know how this concert would play out. I was completely surprised when ninety percent of the population and many staff attended the event. The concert was fantastic. The singer and band played for two solid hours. Most of the inmates and female staff that attended were mesmerized by the singer's really good impersonation of Elvis Presley and his collection of songs. The inmates were singing along to many of the songs. It's funny, but I suspect that a number of inmates were so caught up in the concert they forgot for a short time that they were in prison!

I was really impressed with the singer and his band. After the concert, he signed autographs and talked to interested inmates. I invited the singer and band members to join me and the inmates for supper in the dining room. Looking back, it was one of the most positive days of my wardenship.

Many inmates in prison who were serving long sentences missed human contact with the outside world. Looking back, I suspect that Johnny Cash's concerts in the California prisons in the sixties helped open doors for entertainers to perform inside prisons. I recall another successful concert at the prison, in May 1980, but with a different ending. One Thursday night, I had taken my wife to a Dan Hill concert at the local concert hall. Dan Hill was a successful black Canadian Grammy Award singer and songwriter in the eighties with many number one hits. I approached Dan Hill after the concert and invited him to perform at the prison. He told me that he didn't have time this week but if I phoned his manager he was sure a date could be arranged. Two weeks later, on a Friday afternoon, Dan Hill came to the prison and gave an excellent concert to a very appreciative audience.

After the concert, Dan signed autographs and talked freely with interested inmates.

I approached him and said there was a group of inmates who never had a chance to take in a concert in the gym. I asked him if he would sing and entertain inmates in protective custody and segregation proper. Dan agreed. I contacted the AW Security and made arrangements for Dan to perform with his guitar in segregation in twenty minutes' time. At the time, segregation was almost full. All the inmates were properly dressed.

Dan entertained the ladies in segregation for forty-five minutes. There was something magical in segregation that day. All the inmates were crying when he sang his hit song, "Sometimes When We Touch." Dan received a loud and appreciative applause when he finished. It was the only time I allowed a singer to perform in segregation. Most times, the inmates in segregation were very upset about something in their lives and would not be receptive to a male singer's walking around performing. Dan had been told of the risks. I told him if inmates started to perform or caused problems, we would exit very quickly. But there were no problems. The inmates in protective custody and segregation all acted responsibly that day. After the concert, I invited Dan to my house for dinner and to meet my family. I was happy that he brought his guitar with him and he sang some songs for my wife and small children and then played our piano.

Those times when I brought gifted singers into the prison were invariably the most rewarding days of my correctional working life. Each time I arranged for entertainers to perform in the prison, it was pure magic to see the humanity and smiles on the faces of both inmates and staff. Happiness and good times were usually absent from those who walked inside and experienced the day-to-day existence in a hostile environment.

Frank's Story

Looking back, I am appreciative to Frank W. Anderson, my first-year field supervisor during my Masters of Social Work program in Calgary in 1969. It was Frank's determination that convinced me that adult corrections was the career path I should follow. As previously stated, Frank Anderson had spent fifteen years in Saskatchewan Penitentiary for murder. He was so different from my other professors at the university. He had the intellect and knowledge of the other professors, but his approach to problem solving was infectious because of his low-key style and his very supportive way with his students. Although Frank did not share his unique background with me or other students at the time, there was a sense that he wanted to give something back to corrections because of his successes. Lassoing two students like Pat and myself to enter adult corrections as a career seemed to Frank like penance for the sorrow of his past sins. Nevertheless, I acknowledge his impact on my future role as a warden.

Frank was the first inmate in over 100 years to receive a high school diploma while incarcerated at Saskatchewan Penitentiary. Frank was convicted on October 3, 1936, of murder and sentenced to hang on January 8, 1937. He had killed a guard while attempting to escape from a provincial jail. On December 11, 1936, Frank W. Anderson received a reprieve. Because of his young age, the Minister of Justice agreed that a life sentence would be appropriate. Frank was admitted to Saskatchewan Penitentiary on December 14, 1936.[11]

During Frank's first two years, he was segregated with other young inmates while he slowly matured and was ready to enter the unreal world and belly of a maximum security prison. It wasn't long after admission that the warden at the time and supportive staff realized that Frank had the intelligence and motivation to pursue higher education. Frank revealed that the warden had made him an offer that changed his world. Shortly after being admitted and placed in a separate area with other young inmates, the warden told Frank that if he finished high school, he would help him to get into university.[12]

While incarcerated, Frank learned other skills that helped prepare him for his future employment following release from prison. He initially worked in the stores area and later was transferred to the chief trade instructor's office. He received excellent

---

11 Frank Anderson, *Up the Latter* (Saskatoon: The Gopher Press, 1979), 88.
12 Ibid., 89.

support from his educated supervisor, who was a mechanical engineer and draftsman. Frank completed the financial budget reports for the entire department as well as other departments. His bookkeeping skills would be helpful following his release.[13]

After Frank finished high school, the warden made good and helped him to take correspondence courses from the University of Saskatchewan. It wasn't easy for Frank to take university courses behind bars at that time without the ongoing support of someone who knew the ropes. There were only two staff members at the prison who had university training. Frank completed all the coursework for his Bachelor of Arts degree minus two science courses that he could not take because they required lab work.[14]

After a number of refusals, Frank finally received a Ticket of Leave from the Remission Service. He had support from the warden and other staff who knew him and his special case. It was hard to convince the Remission Service to release a man who had killed a correctional officer. Frank left Saskatchewan Penitentiary in the spring of 1951. He lived in Saskatoon and completed the two lab science courses he needed to receive his university degree. He worked doing bookkeeping for a number of trucking firms. A few years later, Frank moved to Calgary and while there he volunteered with the John Howard Society.[15]

In 1955, Frank married a supportive woman who was willing to help him follow his dreams. Like me, Frank was drawn towards a career of helping people. He wanted to become a professional social worker. He applied to several schools and was accepted at the University of Toronto. Frank and his wife moved east. They had little money. Frank's wife got a job, but her salary was not enough to pay all the bills. After completing his first year, Frank got a job during the summer months as a caseworker with a firm at the train station that helped travellers. During Frank's second year, a female professor who was one of the few faculty staff who knew of his previous prison record suggested that he apply for the government of Ontario training grant for second-year students. The only obligation was to work in corrections anywhere in

13   Ibid., 119.
14   Ibid.
15   Ibid., 176.

Canada. Only two students applied, and they were both successful. Frank finished his Masters of Social Work degree in 1957 and returned to Calgary. He got a job with the John Howard Society working with ex-inmates. It is kind of ironic, but as stated previously, Frank encouraged me to apply for the Solicitor General's Scholarship during the second year of my Masters of Social Work degree. The only obligation was that I work anywhere in Canada in corrections. We both were encouraged to apply for a financial grant by a faculty member and agreed to work in adult corrections.[16]

Frank worked for the John Howard Society for a number of years and then went into private practice. Later he worked for several youth detention centres and in 1967 he taught students at a college in Calgary. In 1969, Frank became a field instructor at the School of Social Welfare in Calgary, Alberta. Frank was my first-year field instructor. My placement was at Woods Christian Homes and at the Calgary Rehabilitation and Research Institute.

When I graduated in 1971, I did not talk to Frank again until early 1980, when I briefly spoke to him on the phone in Vancouver. Frank's background fascinated me. Our paths did not converge until later that year.

In early September 1980, I was sitting at my desk daydreaming and glancing periodically outside the window. I watched motor vehicles enter the parking lot and people exiting to attend meetings in the Correctional Service of Canada building located at one end of the lot. Others were coming to the Prison for Women. I watched two middle-aged adults, a man and a woman, carrying briefcases, walking up the sidewalk towards the front entrance to the prison. I did not recognize the woman but I was very positive that the man was Frank W. Anderson, my former field supervisor at university. Yes! Yes! It was Frank!

I thought he must be coming to visit me. After the two visitors entered the institution and their identification papers were inspected by the staff, I approached them and introduced myself.

---

16 Ibid., 183.

"Welcome to the Prison for Women. It has been a long time since I have seen you. You're looking good. Who is your friend and what brings you to the prison today?"

Frank shook my hand and said he and Mrs. White were members of the National Parole Board and were here to see three inmates that day. I was totally surprised. I didn't say anything at first, since I was not sure his partner was aware of his prison record. I invited them into my office and we spoke for fifteen minutes. I was aware that Parole Board members were coming to the prison that day, but Frank's presence was unbelievable. I asked the two members to drop into my office before exiting the institution.

I was so excited to witness Frank come through the front door as a National Parole Board member! I mentioned to him that the hearings were upstairs in the chapel on the third floor. "One of the classification officers will assist you today. If you need anything, please have one of the officers call me."

He responded, "Thank you, George."

After my two visitors left my office, I sat down on the sofa and thought about what I had witnessed. Frank must be the first—and probably the last—ex-inmate who had served a life sentence in a penitentiary for murdering a guard and ended up being appointed to the Parole Board of Canada. Frank was sentenced to hang, but he lived and was now a full-time National Parole Board member from the Prairie Region.

The Parole Service was established to carry out the work formerly completed by the Remission Service. It was a bold decision by the Prime Minister of Canada and his Cabinet to screen Frank's name in as a candidate for the Parole Board. Frank was interviewed by the Solicitor General and approved to be on the board—truly a remarkable decision that gives hope to all inmates. And Frank did the National Parole Board proud.

After Frank and Mrs. White went upstairs to conduct their parole hearings, I telephoned the classification department and was advised that the Parole Board members were seeing three inmates. The first inmate was Sue, twenty-six years old, from Manitoba, sentenced to four years for arson and theft. Sue was a first-time offender who had gotten caught up in a family dispute.

Prison for Women entrance, 1965;
the chapel takes up the third floor.

Sue and a young female minor burned down a car repair garage that they entered one night to stay warm and drink their beer. Sue fell asleep while smoking. The cigarette burned a hole in the sofa and nearby papers caught on fire. The two young women also stole some money from the till as the building burned. Sue was granted parole to live with her grandmother.

Each month when the National Parole Board conducted hearings, a number of inmates who were friends of the inmate being interviewed by the board, or others that were curious bystanders, all waited outside the chapel for the verdict. The waiting inmates gathered like expectant parents for the news of a newborn baby. Sometimes there were loud cheers and other times, when an inmate received a bump, there was silence and tears. Negative decisions seemed to travel through the institution faster than the speed of light. Decisions for lifers and other inmates with long sentences held the greatest interest. Parole Board hearing days were always the centre of discussion at the morning meal.

The second inmate who was seen by the Parole Board that day was Diane, a thirty-nine-year-old fraud artist or, as they are called, a "paper hanger." Diane was serving her third sentence of three years for writing numerous cheques on her employers' industrial accounts. The Parole Board took twenty-five minutes to issue their verdict. Diane was denied parole. There was no evidence that she had changed and learned her lesson. Silence prevailed when Diane exited the hearing. No tears. Diane knew she had a weak case. She was back working in the kitchen within minutes of the decision. Water off a duck's back. No emotion and no pain.

The third inmate who was seen that day was a twenty-eight-year-old first-time offender named Joan serving a life sentence for killing a female worker in a youth detention centre when Joan was eighteen years old. It was a failed escape attempt. That day there should have been a third member to review the lifer's parole application. The third member remained in the hotel room with a bad case of stomach pain. This was a difficult case. Joan had a history of violence as a juvenile and also had a serious addiction problem. There was some evidence that she had improved her life, but many questions remained. Joan came from a poor family in a bad area of Toronto where alcohol and drug abuse were common. Her parents had both served jail sentences for robbery. She had no marketable skills and her employment opportunities were not good. But she was young and needed a break.

The classification officer was supportive for day parole, but had serious concerns. Mrs. White voted for day parole. It was difficult for Frank, given his parallel background. The hearing went on for one hour and twenty minutes. Frank looked Joan in the eye and said that he was sorry but he thought she was not ready to be released. He suggested that she participate in the AA program. One of his concerns was that Joan had been caught with drugs about five months previously. He voted to deny the day parole. Within two weeks a third member voted on Joan's case. Joan was denied day parole.

Later I spoke to the board members briefly. Frank said it was a difficult board. I observed that he had a small tear at the corner of his eye. I suspect he was thinking about his first meeting with the Ticket of Leave representative and his first denial while at Saskatchewan Penitentiary.

During the early eighties, I had further contact with Frank, as my family travelled west on holidays. On several occasions, I telephoned him while I was in Saskatoon and met him for coffee or lunch in nearby cafés. Our paths would converge again in the first week of 1987. Frank was writing a book on women who had been hanged since Confederation and wanted help to track down some information on several inmates that were granted reprieve from hanging. Frank telephoned me and also wrote a letter outlining his special request, identifying five or six names of inmates that he wanted information on. He promised to send me a copy of his book when it was finished.

Approximately ten years later, I was at work at Regional Headquarters and listening to CBC radio. The female interviewer introduced her guest as Frank W. Anderson, author of a new book on female inmates in Canada who were sentenced to hang. I listened with great interest. I picked up the telephone and left a message for Frank, asking him where my book was. A few weeks later I received from Frank a box in the mail, dated July 1997, containing his book (*A Dance with Death*). Frank's story and his friendship have been an inspiration to me over the years.

Death of an Inmate in Segregation

In early December 1983, Mary Ann experienced a terrible event. A young Native woman named Shirley was placed in segregation for serious intoxication. For three days, she was stoned on something. The security staff suspected that she was removing pills that were concealed in her body cavity. On the fourth night, at 11:55 p.m., a correctional officer making her rounds found Shirley hanging by the neck from the bars in her cell. She had used her bedsheet, ripping it and placing it around her neck. When the correctional officer found Shirley hanging, she yelled to her partner to bring the key and a knife. The two officers cut Shirley down and removed the sheet from her neck. They placed Shirley on the corridor floor. One officer started CPR while the other officer ran to the telephone and called the nurse, asking her to call an ambulance and to come quickly because an inmate had been found hanging and had a weak pulse.

The Duty Correctional Supervisor was notified of the incident and came quickly to segregation. The inmates in PC and in segregation knew something was wrong. The correctional officers were raising their voices. The nurse entered segregation within two minutes and took over CPR from the correctional officer. Shirley's colour was bluish red. I was notified at 11:58 p.m. and arrived within minutes. I asked the Duty Correctional Supervisor to notify the regional duty officer. The nurse called the institutional physician. She reported that Shirley had no pulse and was cyanotic. The ambulance arrived and after paramedics examined the inmate they also found no pulse. The institutional physician arrived within fifteen minutes and pronounced the inmate dead. The police arrived to control the scene. Within half an hour, the coroner and the police identification officers arrived. The prison chaplain was called in and requested to contact the next of kin and inform them of Shirley's death.

All the visitors had to pass through the protective custody area to get into the segregation area. They returned the same way. Before Shirley's body was removed, the Duty Correctional Supervisor advised me that the chairperson of the Native Sisterhood had lobbied to conduct a smudge ceremony over the body. After the coroner cleared the body for removal, I approved the inmate sisterhood leader to light sweet grass and direct the smoke over the body. Because Shirley was Native and a member of the sisterhood, the smudge ceremony helped the Native inmates to deal with her death.

The removal of the young inmate's body inside the black body bag was performed with dignity. The funeral home representatives carried the body out of segregation quickly. When Shirley's body was passing through, there was complete silence. I was told later by a corrections officer that after the authorities exited the scene area, all the inmates in protective custody and segregation had shed a few tears. The next day, I arranged for the psychologist to interview each inmate in segregation, as well as the correctional officers who were involved, to ensure they were okay.

I talked to Mary Ann the next day at her cell. Shirley's death had greatly affected her. She played classical piano music the entire day. Mary Ann told the correctional officers that she was not feeling well and could not tutor inmates that day. She explained that Shirley's death had caught her off-guard. She felt sadness enter her being. Mary Ann remarked that Shirley's death had been a wake-up call and forced her to realize how precious and vulnerable each inmate was in segregation. Mary Ann was stoic with her emotions. I spent only a few minutes with her, since she needed time to heal. Later in the afternoon, the prison chaplain conducted a ceremony for Shirley that was attended by interested inmates and staff.

The investigating police officer advised me a few days later that they had found a suicide note in Shirley's cell. Shirley had reported that she could no longer live without her parents, who had been killed in a house fire two years previously.

The death of an inmate in prison is difficult for staff and inmates alike. When an inmate dies in segregation, it is even more tragic and sorrowful. Every time an inmate dies in prison, the Correctional Service of Canada conducts an internal investigation. It was mandatory that the coroner conduct a community inquest into the death of an inmate to determine if there were issues that might have been dealt with to prevent the death.

Within a short time, it was Christmas again. Mary Ann had experienced her fourth Christmas in prison. Christmas was probably the most difficult time for inmates who did not receive a temporary absence release or did not receive visits. Mary Ann received no pass and had no visits.

4

Ginger's Nightmare

The months went by too quickly, and soon it was the spring of 1984. I experienced a strange event that I still remember this day. In early April, I was advised by the sentence administrator that a federal inmate named Ginger, who had been convicted of fraud, had not been transferred as required to the Prison for Women, but instead had gone from the Toronto West Detention Centre to the Toronto East General Hospital. At first glance, this matter did not register any alarm bells. About three weeks later while visiting the institutional Health Care Centre, Mrs. Thomas, the Chief of Health Care, told me that her health care budget was being adversely affected because she was paying for hospital costs related to a federal inmate at the Toronto East General Hospital. After I made some inquiries to the sentence administrator, I learned that Ginger was the girlfriend of a wealthy man who owned a professional football team. The Chief of Health Care told me that she had received a bill from the Toronto East General Hospital making it clear that Ginger had been assigned a private room and was receiving many costly medical tests. Mrs. Thomas stressed that we must have Ginger transferred to the Prison for Women.

I contacted the warden at the Toronto West Detention Centre and was advised that her prison physician had been contacted by Ginger's boyfriend's doctor to the effect that Ginger was ill, and he needed to perform a number of tests. I smelled something fishy. I contacted the Assistant Chief Crown Attorney for Toronto and asked her to arrange for Ginger's transfer to the Prison for Women. Later that day, I received telephone calls from the chaplain and a medical doctor associated with Toronto East General Hospital informing me that Ginger was too ill to be transported to Kingston. The next day, I learned that Ginger had been moved to a very expensive room and was being treated by several medical specialists. I later learned that Ginger's boyfriend/common-law partner was on the board of the Toronto East General Hospital and that he had made substantial donations to the hospital.

Two days passed before I received a call one morning from a senior staff member representing a senior Liberal Member of Parliament. The man was cordial and well spoken. He advised me that Ginger's boyfriend had contacted his political boss to see if there was something that could be done to keep Ginger in the hospital. It was a strange telephone call. I told the man that Ginger was a federal inmate and had to be transferred to the Prison for Women. After this call, I telephoned the Assistant Crown Attorney and said that we needed to have Ginger transferred immediately.

The next morning, I was advised by Mrs. Thomas that inmate Ginger had been transported via private jet to Kingston the previous night and admitted into Hotel Dieu Hospital. The problem here was that the Prison for Women would be responsible again for Ginger's medical care at the community hospital. Mrs. Thomas further explained that the institutional physician was not in the picture. He had no knowledge of Ginger and did not have her medical files. The light bulb went on brightly. Mrs. Thomas and I suspected Ginger, who was middle-aged and well connected, could not handle being locked up at a maximum security prison. Her wealthy boyfriend was doing his best to keep Ginger in the hospital as the days ticked towards her release. Ginger had been sentenced to three years for fraud relating to a golf course south of Toronto owned by her boyfriend. It was possible that she had taken the rap instead of her wealthy boyfriend.

Once again, I telephoned the Assistant Crown Attorney and asked her to have Ginger, along with her files, transferred to the Prison for Women.

The next day, Ginger was transported by ambulance to the Prison for Women. It was a strange event. Ginger was tucked away in a stretcher with blankets covering her head. I watched the ambulance drivers delivering our prize to the prison. Once inside the foyer, all hell broke out. Having an office close to the front door, I heard Ginger yelling out loud and acting crazy. She was yelling that she was ill and that she should not be admitted to the Prison for Women. She shouted that she was not guilty and felt ill. The ambulance drivers did not know what to do.

Mrs. Thomas was called and came downstairs. She checked over the medical file and found the waiver that stated Ginger was free of infectious disease. Mrs. Thomas could find no medical report that clarified what Ginger's medical problems might be. Ginger was instructed to get out of the stretcher and walk upstairs. She got out of the stretcher and threw herself on the floor. She went bananas. Mrs. Thomas called for a nurse, who came down to the site and gave Ginger a needle to help her to relax. Ginger walked up the stairs and was placed in the institutional Health Care Centre overnight. The next day, the doctor reviewed Ginger's medical file and examined her. He found nothing wrong with her. Her illness appeared to be psychosomatic. Ginger was assigned a cell on "B" range. She was referred to the psychiatrist.

Ginger was a spoiled woman who got whatever she wanted. Her high-profile boyfriend had served a previous sentence for fraud and was known to correctional authorities.

Ginger made sure I was aware of her relationship with her boyfriend. Sometimes when she spoke I received the impression that Ginger thought her boyfriend was "God." Ginger saw the psychiatrist several weeks later and was treated for mild depression. She told me her boyfriend was well connected to my political masters in Ottawa and that she would be out of the prison shortly. Her appeal on her conviction and sentence was dismissed. I found her to be a nice lady at times, but she was definitely totally out of her depth in the Prison for Women. She was a fraud artist. I viewed her as a phony, somewhat shallow person interested only in her own welfare.

Ginger was right about one thing. She emphasized that she would be granted parole on the day she was eligible. True to form, she was released on day parole the day she was eligible. Ginger was a woman you would never forget. If she had had her way, she would have served her entire sentence in a hospital suite and been treated like a queen. A few years later, I read in the Toronto papers with interest the story of Ginger's battling adversaries over her dead boyfriend's estate.

Pamala's Ordeal

Sometimes inmates bring up old memories and stories that surprise you about where they have been. I recall interviewing an inmate named Pamala in 1979 who was doing fifteen years for trafficking in heroin. Pamala, who was in her early forties, resided in Vancouver. Pamala told me that she had been using drugs for many years. Her own mother was a heroin addict and had served time at the Prison for Women in the late fifties and early sixties. At one time, her mother helped finance her drug habit by working as a backyard abortionist. She received two years, five months for this activity.

Pamala came to my office many times trying to make sense of her sentence and addiction to heavy drugs. Although she always seemed wired and high-strung, at times she made a lot of sense.

Pamala trusted me and shared her secrets. One day she asked to see me. When she entered my office, she asked if it was okay to smoke. Pamala loved to smoke cigarettes and drink coffee from a mug. I asked Pamala what was on her mind. Many previous sessions I had had with Pamala centred on her heroin addiction. Pamala spoke clearly. She said, "Last night I had a flashback going back ten years. I remembered being involved in an experimental program at the prison that was to help me overcome my serious drug addiction." I asked her what she remembered. "Well, I recollect the psychiatrist giving me drugs to help me."

I responded, "What drugs?"

"The psychiatrist gave me LSD and another drug called scoline. One drug made me relax while the other drug made me dizzy, and I experienced awful hallucinations."

I asked her, "How long did you participate in the program?"

Pamala thought about the question and said, "I think it was five or six months." Pamala left my office crying and saying the program had not helped her.

In previous decades, CSC completed research programs with very little supervision. In the fifties and sixties, research programs like the LSD experiments were initiated without close supervision or control. Inmates were selected to participate without signing any liability or consent forms. Looking back there appeared to be no evidence that there were medical doctors, psychiatrists, or professional associations overseeing what was happening in the Prison for Women.

At the time of my tenure as warden, medical directors at regional and national headquarters supervised medical research activities in all federal institutions. Individual doctors, psychologists, and psychiatrists required willing inmates to sign release forms giving their consent, and their research proposals had to be approved in advance before proceeding. There was a great deal of care and concern for the inmates as participants, and ethical standards were followed.

A number of years later, I read several articles in Canadian national newspapers reporting that an inmate sued CSC for involving her in LSD research programs in Montreal many years ago without her consent. I suspected that the legal case was probably settled out of court. I believe administrators employed for CSC are very aware today of the professional standards and requirements when involving willing inmate participants. Looking back, Pamala did participate in a research program, but did not realize, or was not advised of, the possible long-term consequences of this research. Today CSC has improved its standards and has set firm guidelines to protect inmates.

During the latter part of 1984, Mary Ann had completed all her high school courses and, in addition, she had completed three college correspondence courses and received excellent marks. One day when I was visiting the protective custody area, the schoolteacher and Mary Ann's classification officer were leaving her cell area. Mary Ann seemed very happy. That day she had applied for day parole to attend St. Lawrence College in Kingston. Mary Ann would be eligible for day parole in six months. Her classification officer and teacher were both supportive of her application. Having some curiosity, I asked Mary Ann, "What course of study are you interested in?"

Mary Ann looked up at me and showed me the college program book. She elaborated, "I am very interested in taking the architecture technologist two-year program. The program requires good math and drawing skills."

I looked at Mary Ann and said, "Go for it, girl."

As I was leaving, Mary Ann increased the volume of her favourite opera, *Madame Butterfly*. She was excited and ready to tackle the world.

School and Post-Secondary Education

During the latter part of 1984, the number of lifers and inmates with long sentences of over seven years reached a new high. One day, the Inmate Sentence Administrator told me that we had forty-two inmates that were serving long sentences, including thirty-five that were serving a life sentence. Many of the inmates joined a self-help group called Ten Plus. Of the lifer group, six inmates were serving life sentences for first-degree murder. These inmates were not eligible for parole until they had served twenty-five years. In 1976, the death sentence was abolished. Inmates convicted of first-degree murder would normally have been sentenced to hang. Given the number of inmates serving long sentences, I was always looking for program opportunities to help this group facilitate their sentences and bring more meaning to their lives in prison.

One of the more successful and impressive programs was the school program offered at the prison. In my view, this was the centrepiece of the program opportunities for inmates at the PFW. I was most pleased and honoured to attend special events in the school when inmates received certificates for completing a grade or two, or, having completed their high school education, receiving a diploma. It was so rewarding to see an inmate come to the school who could not read or write, after months, and sometimes years, it was amazing to see the change in the students' progress. In some cases, to witness a given inmate read a book was a positive highlight and experience that stayed in my memory bank.

Given Mary Ann's progress in the school program, and, of course, Frank's previous success and motivation in obtaining a high school and university education while incarcerated, I was biased and offered my full support for these programs. I was very impressed with the school administrators, CSC teachers, contract teachers who taught at the school, student teachers from Queen's University who entered the prison school and taught and tutored students, and many volunteers who shared their time with needy students. These participants who reached out to students offered all of them a great deal.

A select group of qualified inmates serving long sentences completed university courses by correspondence, which served its purpose. Qualified inmates who completed high school had an excellent opportunity to take university courses offered by Queen's University at the Prison for Women and Collins Bay Institution between 1981 and 1991. In some cases, staff members took several university courses along with the inmates in the school at the PFW.

One of the university professors who set up the program at the PFW in 1981 was highly motivated and very supportive of female students taking university courses and expanded the opportunities for them. In 1987, this male professor who was teaching at the PFW helped develop another avenue for students interested in post-secondary education. He developed a program whereby a small group of female students (six or less) were escorted and bused each morning to Collins Bay Institution and participated with male inmates in taking university courses.

After a number months, the university program was stopped for awhile. There was resistance from the guards' union and people in the community who did not like the idea of CSC paying university tuition for inmates. The guards' union was concerned that some female inmates did not dress appropriately when entering a male institution. The program recommenced after some changes were made, but was finally terminated in 1991 after the Conservative government decided it could not support inmates receiving free university courses.

On a personal note, I observed that inmates who participated in university-level courses were less problematic and adjusted better in serving their sentences. I was grateful to the educational administrators, teaching staff, professors, and volunteers who opened a window of opportunity for inmate learning. Their participation helped make this program a success story. The Queen's University professor who was in charge of the program to teach university-level courses to inmates informed the author that approximately 600 male and female students participated in the university program over a ten-year period.

Programs: Mother/Child; Aviary

I was extremely concerned about young women who were entering the prison either pregnant or who had small children. After the government abolished capital punishment, inmates convicted of murder were given long sentences. I remember several young women that either had a young child or were pregnant when they arrived at the prison. During my wardenship, there was no provision for an inmate to keep her child in prison even for a short time. An inmate sentenced to life or receiving a very long sentence either had to place her child with the father, her mother, family, or friends, or adopt out the child; otherwise, the Children's Aid Society would take custody.

In late 1984, a young woman named Francis went into labour at the prison. Francis was serving twenty years for second-degree murder. She had no relatives or friends who were in a position to look after a baby, and then a child, for many years. After fourteen hours of difficult labour, Francis gave birth to a baby girl at the Kingston General Hospital. The prison chaplain and classification officer visited Francis at the hospital. Francis, facing a difficult situation, decided to put her child up for adoption. Francis decided that she would not hold the baby after the birth, fearing it would be too difficult for her to give up the child.

I remember another inmate, of East Indian background, who was serving a life sentence for murder and was housed in the PC area. She had two small children who had been placed with a family hundreds of miles away. As the children grew and became more mature, the guardian foster parent would travel once or twice a year so the children could visit their natural mother. It was not a perfect situation, but provided stability for the children until the mother was released many years down the road.

I tried several times to convince my superiors at Regional Headquarters and National Headquarters to develop a program whereby a mother could care for her new baby for one year, but was unsuccessful. The main reason given to deny the proposal was that there was no physical space to accommodate a number of mothers and infants. After visiting the Purdy Treatment Centre for Women in Washington State, I was convinced that this program for women with small children was something that had to be developed in Canada. I recall having a meeting with the superintendent of the provincial women's prison at Brandon, Manitoba. She started a small program during the eighties that allowed mother and child to reside together in a special area. The inmates serving sentences in provincial jails served relatively short sentences; therefore, it was easier for provincial institutions to manage that kind of program.

It would be many years before the Correctional Service of Canada developed a program that allowed for an inmate to have her child residing with her during the first few formative years.

During the 1996–97 fiscal year, a new position, Deputy Commissioner for Women (Women Offenders Unit), was created at the Correctional Service of Canada by the Solicitor General. The new position was filled by a woman to deal with female offenders ("Federally Sentenced Women").

In 1990, it had been recommended by women's groups to develop a mother/child program. In July 1996, a pilot mother/child program was started at the Healing Lodge in Alberta. In 1998, the program was gradually introduced into several new regional women's institutions across Canada.

On February 27, 2003, a comprehensive Commissioner's Directive (CD 768) entitled *Mother/Child Program* was signed by the then Commissioner of the Correctional Service of Canada.[17]

In terms of Program Eligibility, Paragraph 17 of the CD states that "only women classified as minimum or medium security and who are housed in institutions that offer the program are eligible to participate."[18]

At the time of this writing (April 2008), there are four inmates that have children with them between newborn and one

---

17 *Commissioner's Directive 768, Mother/Child Program*, Correctional Service of Canada, 2003.

18 Ibid., 62.

year of age at Grand Valley Institution (Ontario), Joliette Institution (Quebec), and Fraser Valley Institution (British Columbia). There are two part-time mother/child arrangements in three institutions across Canada.

For some inmates that meet all the criteria and requirements, the mother/child program can be a very positive program opportunity for both mother and child.

Having so many lifers in the population, I was eager to find the right program to benefit the group. I thought I had the program that inspired by motivation. One day while driving north of Kingston with my family, we came across a sign that said Aviary Care and Research Centre. I remembered a year before I had taken an injured blackbird to the centre. I was curious and decided to introduce myself. I learned that the lady running the centre was a nurse and was very passionate about wild birds. Injured wild birds were dropped off at the centre all year long. Some injured birds were delivered from locations seventy miles away. At the Aviary Care Centre there were many birds, including eagles, owls, hawks, blue jays, robins, crows, and many other species. The Aviary Centre received donations from the public to help support the program. I was very impressed by the program and the great care the birds received. Sometimes local veterinarians would call the operator of the centre and ask her if she could care for a sick bird that had been brought to the animal hospital.

During the next three weeks, I made many inquiries about how one could set up a wild bird aviary centre. I contacted a young local veterinarian who taught part time at St. Lawrence College. She was very interested in helping to set up a program in the prison. She had some knowledge of wild birds and was willing to teach inmates. I was referred to another veterinarian who taught at the Veterinary College at Guelph, Ontario. This professor was an expert on wild birds and was prepared to oversee the program if I obtained funding from national headquarters. The operator of the local aviary where I had visited was also prepared to assist where possible.

I identified a location in the prison where a bird enclosure could be constructed. I started to work on the proposal. I decided to call a special meeting of interested lifers and inmates serving long sentences who might be interested in working at a wild bird aviary. Fourteen lifers and other inmates with long sentences came to the special meeting. The young female veterinarian was my guest. The inmates were very interested in the program and asked many questions. I explained that sometimes an ill bird would have to be put down when it was too ill or suffering. I told the inmates that the nurse and veterinarian would be responsible for this task. The inmates were upset and said that if they were trained, they should be able to put injured birds down as well. After the meeting, the veterinarian told me that setting up firm guidelines and control of narcotics was essential; also that it was unlikely approval would be obtained from the government authorities if inmates were handling narcotics.

Given the strong reaction from the inmates, I could not support the program with inmates using narcotics to put ill birds down. I worked hard to get this program off the ground. I was prepared to do whatever it took to get the program started. I never thought that inmates would feel so strongly about using narcotics to put ill birds down. Looking over the background of the fourteen inmates that came to the meeting, I observed that ten of them had serious substance abuse issues.

Sometimes good ideas for interesting programs never get off the ground. I was very frustrated that I could not get this program started. I learned something that day. A good idea requires a lot of research and planning, and finally the inmates must be consulted to determine their concerns and level of interest.

Soon it was Christmas of 1984. Mary Ann was experiencing her fifth Christmas at the prison. There were seven inmates in protective custody at the time. There were four inmates, including Mary Ann, serving a life sentence for offences against children. There were also three other inmates serving long sentences involving children. I quickly visited Mary Ann and the other inmates in segregation on Christmas morning. Mary Ann was lying on her bed and listening to a beautiful classical concerto performed by Glenn Gould. When I approached Mary Ann's cell, she said that she had applied for day parole and hoped 1985 would be a good year. Looking back now, I realize Mary Ann did in fact experience a special event in 1985 that changed her life at the prison. More about this later.

The Semiahmoo Six Group

Although no inmate escaped from the prison during my wardenship, there was an event that helped create more control and tightened the security of the institution. In mid-1984, I received information that we were expecting the arrival of two female members of the Semiahmoo Six, a self-styled urban guerrilla group operating in British Columbia. The Semiahmoo Six were arrested on November 22, 1982, on the Squamish Highway by members of the RCMP Tactical Unit dressed as highway maintenance employees.

The Semiahmoo Six were very active in terrorist activities in Canada. On May 30, 1982, the Semiahmoo Six were responsible for bombing the BC Hydro Cheekeye Dunsmuir Substation on Vancouver Island. In October 1982, this group bombed the Litton System Factory in Toronto. The Litton factory manufactured guidance electronics systems for the cruise missile. The RCMP suspected this group was also involved in other criminal activities. They had strong suspicions that the Semiahmoo Six might be linked to the Baader-Meinhop gang (RAF),[19] another urban terrorist group operating in West Germany. A Special O Squad (observation unit) provided surveillance of this group for several months before they were finally arrested.[20]

Under the circumstances, we felt it was necessary to perform a total review of our security system at the prison. The sally port entrance was changed. All vehicles had to pass through two separate electronic gates once inside the sally port. Our security relationship with nearby Kingston Penitentiary was also enhanced. Additional electronic surveillance cameras were installed. The

---

19 The Baader-Meinhop gang in Germany was the original name; later, in the seventies and eighties, it was referred to as the Red Army Faction or *Rote Armee Faktion*—RAF.

20 *The Vancouver Sun*, "RCMP Eyes Stalked Gang for Two Months" (June 9, 1984), A12.

staff practised new security drills. The end result was that the security of the prison was greatly enhanced.

When we received the two female members of the Semiahmoo Six, they probably did not know that their group was responsible for the increase in security at the prison. Thirty-year-old Ruth was considered to be one of the leaders of the Semiahmoo Six. She was sentenced to life imprisonment. The younger woman, named Joann, was twenty-three years old and somewhat naïve. She received twenty years for her involvement with the group. Several males of the group, including Ruth's common-law husband, were housed at Millhaven Institution, a maximum security prison located about twenty miles from the Prison for Women.

There was no question that Ruth was one of the leaders. I found her to be an extremely intelligent woman who was anti-establishment and a committed terrorist. Ruth caused no serious problems at the prison; however, she used her intellect to move the inmate agenda. I don't know what happened to Ruth as a young child, but in my opinion it was shameful that her talents were misguided. Ruth was one of the brightest inmates I ever encountered at the prison. She had made choices in her life and would always have to bear the weight of her past decisions. Ruth could have achieved a great deal; instead, she settled for the life of a failed activist.

There was one unusual event related to the Semiahmoo Six that I will never forget. After several years into Ruth's sentence, she applied for a private family visit (PFV) with her common-law husband at Millhaven Institution. The PFV was approved and was uneventful. Approximately six months later, Ruth again applied for a PFV with her husband at the Prison for Women. The PFV was approved for a weekend, two weeks later. One day, I received a visit from a very attractive agent of the Canadian Security Intelligence Service (CSIS). The agent carried a locked briefcase attached to a chain around her wrist. After introducing herself, the agent said, "We are interested in the Semiahmoo Six inmates." The agent opened her briefcase and showed me a warrant signed by a Federal Court Judge to conduct electronic surveillance on Ruth and her common-law husband during the next family visit in the little house. The agent would not leave me a copy of the warrant. I telephoned the Regional Manager of Security and asked for his advice. Within fifteen minutes, he returned the telephone call and said that the warrant was legal. I suspected that because one or more of the Semiahmoo Six had been to West Germany, the RCMP and Canadian Security Intelligence Service (CSIS) thought maybe they were connected to the Baader-Meinhop gang. This was the only time as a warden I experienced this kind of attention.

Ruth and Joann were eventually released on parole. I felt that both ladies had had enough of urban terrorist activities.

Private family visiting house, 1981.
(Courtesy Corrections Service Canada Museum)

Mentally Ill Inmates

One of the problems facing administrators of female institutions was the lack of facilities and programs to manage inmates who suffered from mental health issues. The prison had its own unique internal stressors that adversely affected a normal person, let alone an inmate with mental health symptoms. It took its toll on female inmates serving very long sentences, especially young women trying to make sense of their new lives. Depression was a common illness for lifers. Periodically, an inmate with a history of mental health issues suffered a meltdown at the PFW.

During the late seventies and early eighties, I was fortunate in having several options to manage these inmates. At any given time, the PFW had twenty-five to thirty-five inmates who really required mental health services. During the period between 1975 and 1986, mentally ill inmates sought and received counselling from the psychologist, chaplain, physician, nurses, psychiatrist, and their own classification officer. In addition, mental health and addiction counsellors from the community entered the prison and involved inmates in AA (Alcoholics Anonymous) and NA (Narcotics Anonymous) programs. I observed that a number of inmates who had mental health issues had addiction problems as well and sometimes had medical problems to complicate matters.

When an inmate exhibited mental health problems, the normal route was to have her seen by the institutional physician and then, if needed, referred to the psychiatrist or psychologist. If the inmate did not respond, we had several options. If she was too depressed or exhibited serious mental health symptoms, sometimes in rare instances we were able to transfer her to the Kingston Psychiatric Hospital for intensive day counselling by various professionals.

From 1979 to the mid-years of the eighties, we were fortunate to be able to refer some inmates with mental health issues to the forensic ward at the St. Thomas Mental Health Hospital located at St. Thomas, Ontario. One of the psychiatrists who worked at National Headquarters had a psychiatrist friend who was the chief of staff at the St. Thomas hospital. He agreed to receive from four to six inmates from the PFW. The primary qualification was that each inmate had to be certifiable as being mentally ill.

Some inmates aggravated their situation by taking psychotropic medications combined with homemade brew and any other illegal drugs they could get their hands on. It was not unusual to have three or four inmates on the waiting list for a transfer to St. Thomas Hospital.

By 1987, changes were occurring in the provincial mental health programs. A number of mental health facilities were being downsized or closed, and forensic beds were significantly reduced. In 1986, only two inmates from the PFW were admitted to St. Thomas Hospital. I had visited the facilities at St. Thomas

Hospital on several occasions during the previous six years to see our inmates, and must admit I was impressed with the hospital staff, facility, and some of the programs offered to our inmates. It was a sad day in 1986 when the current director of the hospital advised me that by the end of 1987, few inmates could be accommodated at the hospital because of budget cutbacks.

The same year, the director of the Regional Treatment Centre agreed to take, for a short time, some inmates who were experiencing behavioural problems, but would not take inmates that were very aggressive or seriously mentally ill. The nearby Treatment Centre accepted five or six inmates. This arrangement provided the staff with an excellent resource to manage selected inmates. This helped a little bit, but a real problem emerged. Inmates with serious mental health diagnoses overwhelmed the sole psychiatrist. I suspected that a good percentage of the inmates with mental health issues were receiving psychotropic medications. The staff managed as best they could, but when an inmate exhibited overly aggressive or unpredictable behaviour, a placement in segregation was the only viable method of control available. A warden may confine an offender to involuntary segregation when there are reasonable grounds to believe that the offender might jeopardize or put at risk the security of the institution and/or the safety of other inmates or staff. In addition, involuntary segregation may be necessary if the inmate is personally at risk. The safety and security of the institution sometimes necessitated involuntary placement in segregation. There were no other institutions to accommodate a difficult inmate. The staff had to manage the problem at the prison.

I saw the future and was concerned. Provincial governments across Canada were moving to downsize mental health facilities. Fewer and fewer forensic beds were available. I suspected this situation would only get worse.

Mary Jo's Story

Over the years, the staff encountered some inmates that required all the mental health services. I remember an inmate named Mary Jo, who was the first inmate sentenced as a dangerous offender. I first met Mary Jo when she arrived at the prison in 1977. She was a very hyperactive nineteen-year-old white female who had numerous scars on her face, arms, and legs. She spoke quickly and became defensive easily. Mary Jo was first sentenced to six years for abduction and six other charges related to taking a female correctional officer hostage. She had a lengthy juvenile record for assaults and weapons offences. I suspected Mary Jo was neglected as a child, as she always seemed to be looking for attention and reassurance. She was released on Mandatory Supervision in December 1979.

Mary Jo was arrested in early 1980 for assaulting a female escort and sentenced to 150 days and 90 days for theft. She was sent briefly to St. Thomas Psychiatric Hospital for assessment and returned to the Prison for Women. She committed a number of assaults in the prison using a weapon.

In 1982, Mary Jo was escorted weekly for one year to attend therapy sessions with a psychiatrist in the community. Mary Jo was close to getting out on Mandatory Supervision release. She verbally threatened several times to kill me. Although Mary Jo had not been convicted of murder or attempted murder, I myself was convinced that she planned to cause physical harm to me when she was released. She wrote a letter one day stating she would kill me and my family. The letter, which was found in her cell, detailed her intentions and depicted how she would use her knife. The police reviewed her file and written threats to me and were concerned for my safety. Mary Jo was charged by the police with threatening letters with intent to cause death. After the conviction of this charge, the crown attorney used this factor when he applied for the dangerous offender status.

Mary Jo had seen the psychologist, family physician, psychiatrist, and chaplain, but nothing seemed to work. She required a great deal of mental health therapy. Because of Mary Jo's extreme behaviour, she was confined in segregation for six months. She was not mentally ill, but was very aggressive and unpredictable. Under the influence of alcohol or drugs, she could be dangerous.

Mary Jo was again released on Mandatory Supervision in January 1983 after the National Parole Board's failed attempt to "gate" or keep her in prison, and special mental health counsellors were arranged to work with her in the community. In March 1983, Mary Jo was charged with assault against a police officer after she threatened him with a knife. This time the Crown proceeded to declare Mary Jo a dangerous offender. In January 1985, a judge reluctantly declared her a dangerous offender. In June 1985, the Court of Appeal dismissed the Crown's appeal and upheld the judge's order for a six-month sentence.

Looking back, Mary Jo's behaviour became increasingly problematic during the early eighties. She was involved in a number of assaults in the prison using a knife. It was necessary to place her in segregation. She swallowed pieces of glass and vomited up blood. She got hold of a piece of glass or razor blade and cut up her wrists and arms. Every week Mary Jo was escorted to the Health Care Centre and her wounds were treated. Mary Jo had scores of scars on her wrists. This behaviour had been going on for years and had begun when she was first incarcerated as a juvenile.

Another particular behaviour that highlighted Mary Jo was her rocking. Some days in segregation, Mary Jo would sit on the floor and rock back and forth. She would continue with this behaviour for hours at a time. When Mary Jo was extremely upset and erratic, she would throw pieces of flesh from her arm and feces at the staff, and especially at me. Given Mary Jo's condition, the institutional physician arranged for Mary Jo to be assessed at a noted forensic facility near Toronto. Mary Jo was returned to the prison (segregation) after two days with no diagnosis or recommended treatment plan.

One day when I was visiting segregation, Mary Jo heard me talking in the PC area. The door was open to allow the two Salvation Army officers to exit the segregation area. Captain Jones spoke to me briefly as she was leaving the unit. "Warden Caron, I am very concerned about Mary Jo. She has a small piece of glass and is throwing pieces of flesh out of her cell. She is yelling profanities and telling everyone that she is going to kill you. Is there any facility that would accept her? She needs help badly."

I was concerned, commenting, "We have tried to get her into St. Thomas Hospital but they refused to accept her."

During the week, I had a visit from the chaplain, the chairperson of the Citizen's Advisory Committee, a representative of the Federal Correctional Investigator's office, and a local representative of the Elisabeth Fry Society, all expressing concern for Mary Jo. They all asked if there was a facility for Mary Jo. I briefed my boss on my dilemma.

Before the hour was over, I toured the segregation unit. I went from cell to cell, talking to the seven inmates residing there. Mary Jo was in a cell on the ground floor. She started to raise her voice. "Caron, you are a fucking asshole." The staff had placed a large transparent plastic shield that I could use when I passed Mary Jo's cell. As expected, Mary Jo started to throw blood and pieces of flesh from her arm towards me. I heard her yell, "Caron, I am going to kill you for locking me up." I could see she was in medical distress. I could not reach her.

I immediately left the area and called the Chief of Health Care and AW Security and asked them to arrange for two nurses with security backup to enter the cell, treat her wounds, and have the area cleaned of blood. Mary Jo would somehow obtain pieces of glass and a small razor blade wrapped up in plastic and secure them in her body cavity. Because of federal legislation, we were not able to conduct an internal search. Sometimes at night, inmates in nearby cells would arrange to place an item on a string and direct it towards Mary Jo's cell.

Two nurses visited segregation and cleaned Mary Jo's wounds. The institutional physician prescribed a sleeping pill that put Mary Jo into a deep sleep. Mary Jane's arms were in bad shape. I contacted the physician and asked him to see if we could get Mary Jo into St. Thomas. The staff were exhausted. Unfortunately, once again our referral was turned down. The doctor called me later and said that Mary Jo would be sedated for several weeks and placed in a straightjacket if need be. Security staff were going to observe her cell very closely.

On the first day of the second week, Mary Jo asked for a glass of water and wanted to speak to the Chairperson of the Inmate Committee. I approved the visit. The Chair of the Inmate Committee approached me later that day. She asked, "If Mary Jo cleans up her act for two straight weeks with no problems, can she return to the population?" The chair stated that the committee would take turns visiting her cell.

I was without any options. I replied quickly, "If she can clean up her act for two solid weeks I will approve the plan." Two weeks went by with no incidents. Mary Jo was returned to the population and subsequently improved.

About six months later, after I had left the prison in late 1987, Mary Jo was returned to the prison, her MS revoked because of threatening behaviour. Mary Jo was found dead one afternoon on her bed in the Health Care Centre. She had died mysteriously of asphyxiation. Given the number of inmates who had questionable relationships with Mary Jo, it is possible she was murdered by another inmate. Her death was never clarified.

It is possible that if Mary Jo had received proper treatment and care as a juvenile, her life would have been greatly improved. To die in prison under questionable circumstances was a terrible way to lose her life. I wish that I could have reached Mary Jo's inner self and assisted her transformation into a mature young woman.

Having an inmate like Mary Jo took a great deal of emotional strength from the staff to manage her stay at the prison. It was difficult to have an inmate so hurt and vulnerable.

Thank God not all inmates were like Mary Jo.

5

Mary's Story

I clearly remember an inmate named Mary, who was at the opposite end of the spectrum from Mary Jo. Mary was a fifty-three-year-old white inmate who stood five feet four inches tall and had an average weight. She had short brown hair and was always dressed properly. She had an infectious smile and was a pleasure to be near. Mary was a registered nurse by profession and was sentenced to life for killing her daughter's baby. This was such a sad story. Mary was a very devout, moralistic Catholic who practised her religion faithfully. She had a twenty-one-year-old son named Mark and a twenty-three-year-old daughter named Theresa, who attended college in a city close to home.

Mary told me that her daughter had gained some weight at college and thought it was normal. She came home one night and told her mother that she wasn't feeling well. Mary worked as a nurse in the emergency department in a large Catholic hospital. Her husband and son were out of town and not expected back for one week. Theresa went into the bathroom and went into heavy labour. She was in the bathroom for about thirty minutes. Mary, not hearing her daughter, went to find out where she was. She found her daughter in the bathroom on the floor with blood all over her. Beside Theresa was a newborn baby. Theresa had given birth to a six-pound baby girl. Mary was in complete shock. She did not know her daughter was pregnant or that she had been having premarital sex. Theresa had been wearing loose clothing that concealed her pregnancy. She always told her mother that she would not have sex until she was married.

Mary looked at the baby and observed that it was not breathing properly. Mary told the story of how the baby had died and that she could not take the baby to the hospital, since everyone knew her there. She panicked and decided to place it in a blanket and bury the body in the backyard.

Mary was extremely upset and could not face reality. She drove her daughter to another city and had her seen by a doctor. About five days later, a female friend of Theresa's who knew that she was pregnant came to see her and to see the baby. Mary burst into tears and said that the baby was dead and buried in the backyard. Theresa's friend could not believe what she was hearing. The friend was upset and told her mother, who was a policewoman, that Theresa's baby was buried in their backyard.

The next day, the police arrived at Mary's house and dug up the makeshift grave. The police removed the dead body and took the corpse to the morgue where an autopsy was performed. The police were told by the pathologist that the baby had died as result of someone's suffocating it. Theresa was interviewed by the police. She told them that soon after the baby was born, it lapsed into unconsciousness. Mary was later interviewed by the police and admitted that the baby had died, and that she had buried the child in the backyard. Mary was charged and convicted of murder and sentenced to life with no parole opportunity for ten years.

Mary arrived at the PFW in June 1984. She was truly a fish out of water.

Mary was a very pleasant woman who was intelligent and easy to talk with. She had the best lawyer money could buy. Her husband and son were totally surprised by her actions. Her husband mortgaged the family home to obtain funds to cover the expensive legal bills. Mary appealed her conviction, but was unsuccessful. She spoke clearly and softly. She did not hide her disappointment. I met several times with Mary during the first two years of her sentence. Of all the inmates that I encountered at the prison, I would put Mary at the top of the class. It was strange, but I was so impressed by Mary's demeanour and her overall approach to life that I found it difficult to view her as a criminal. In my view, all the inmates were found guilty by the court. Some inmates were more guilty than others. I always felt Mary never told me the full story of her case. I didn't know if she smothered the baby, but initially I was convinced that she was taking the rap for her daughter, who was a senior in college and near graduation.

Mary presented absolutely no problems to the staff. Sometimes privately I wished that Mary were not in prison for murder. I would have hired her on the spot if she had not been involved with the offence of which she had been convicted. Mary was self-confident, intelligent, polite, and communicated freely. She was a mature woman, but her Achilles heel was the fact that she could not face her peers and explain her daughter's pregnancy and giving birth to a child, and the obvious sin against God's commandment and the Church's moral standards.

During the second-last interview I had with Mary, she broke down. Tears rushed out of her eyes and sprinkled the floor. She acknowledged that it was wrong to bury the baby. She never acknowledged responsibility for the child's death.

My hat goes off to Mary's husband. As previously stated, he mortgaged their house to provide funds for a strong legal defence. Each week, he would travel eight hours by automobile to visit his wife. For several years, he would spend the odd weekend with Mary in the Family Visiting Centre.

Mary worked as a tutor in the school and assisted the chaplain. She was granted escorted temporary absences when she was first eligible. In her seventh year at the prison, she was transferred to Isabel McNeill Correctional Centre, across the street from the prison. She worked in the library at the correctional staff college, located a few steps from the prison. Mary was granted full parole on her eligibility date and returned to live with her husband.

The work environment at the PFW was never boring. My horizons were stretched like a rubber band. After a number of years at the PFW, you would think that you would have learned all there was to know about the female offender. During my first few years, I openly admitted that I had a difficult time accepting female homosexual behaviour. At any given time, I suspect that thirty percent of the population was openly gay. Given the long sentences inmates were serving, situational homosexual behaviour was not uncommon. Some inmates with strong sexual desires participated in sexual encounters with confirmed homosexual inmates. During my last six years at the prison, I came to accept this reality. I also realized that when homosexual relationships terminated and dissolved, sometimes the fallout could have disastrous consequences.

I recall a situation in 1982. Two younger women were involved in a serious relationship. Everybody in the prison accepted Carole and Jane as a homosexual pair. After serving five years for robbery with violence, Jane, who was the dominant person in the relationship, was released on Mandatory Supervision. She had a serious drug problem. After six months, she was returned to the PFW. Carole was now involved with a twenty-year-old first-time offender. When I received information that Jane was coming back, I alerted security staff and made sure Jane was placed on "A" range and not in the wing area. After entering the institution, Jane was informed that Carole was with another partner. Jane would have no part of this situation. She waited until evening recreation period, at which time she jumped Carole's new girlfriend as she entered the gymnasium and suddenly slashed her with a shiv (homemade knife) on the side of her head and neck.

Jane was handcuffed by security staff and escorted to segregation after the shiv was secured. The young victim, named Janice, was bleeding profusely. She was taken to the Health Care Centre and treated by a nurse until the ambulance arrived and then transported to an outside hospital; she was admitted to the hospital after receiving emergency surgery. The wounds were deep and seven to eight inches long. Janice sustained serious wounds to the right neck and cheek areas.

The Joint Penitentiary and Police Squad detectives were called in. They interviewed Janice and staff at the prison. Janice told them that she was attacked by Jane for no reason. The police laid an attempted murder charge against Jane. Janice required a second operation after her blood pressure dropped dramatically. After the third night in segregation, Jane ripped up her bedsheets and attempted suicide. The alert security staff cut Jane down and removed the bedsheet strips from around her neck. Jane suffered irreversible brain damage. It was ironic that the victim and attacker were placed in adjacent rooms on the same floor in the outside hospital. Jane's injuries were serious, and she had to be placed in a permanent long-care nursing home. Two years later,

Jane swallowed a bottle of pills and died at age twenty-seven. Institutional gay relationships can be troublesome.

However, in one case, a gay relationship helped two inmates complete their sentences with minimal problems.

Mouse Meets Jamie

In early 1985, Mary Ann was taking a few correspondence courses and continued to work as an inmate tutor. As the weeks passed by, Mary Ann became increasingly anxious waiting for her parole hearing. She had received a letter from the National Parole Board telling her she would be interviewed in the spring. Mary Ann passed her leisure time painting and drawing. She was a good artist and enjoyed drawing pictures of buildings.

During the first week of February 1985, Security arranged for a new inmate cleaner who was considered trustworthy to enter the protective custody area and clean the hallways and bathroom cells. The inmate cleaner's name was Jamie. She was a big woman with strong muscles and great strength. Jamie, who was thirty-one years of age, had been at the prison for seven years and was residing in the wing area. As previously indicated, the wing area was a less secure area where fifty inmates lived in rooms similar to university dorm rooms. Each inmate had her own key to open the wooden door to the room. They all showered and bathed in separate stalls in a large bathroom and used common toilets located in the same general area. They were allowed to decorate their own rooms. Generally, inmates were happy to be living in this area of the prison. It was the preferred living arrangement in the prison. The fifty rooms were always full. Very seldom was a room available.

Jamie was a lesbian and seemed interested in two females living in the protective custody area. Mary Ann reported that initially the correctional staff watched Jamie closely. At first Jamie cleaned every second day. After one month, the staff were satisfied that she posed minimal risk to inmates in protective custody. Each day, Jamie entered the PC range and cleaned the hallways and bathroom. In time, Jamie got to know all the inmates in PC and gained their trust. As the weeks passed, Mary Ann stated that she found herself watching Jamie's movements very closely. Later, they would be a team.

Sometimes when an inmate is locked up for a long period of time, especially an inmate who received very little attention and no visits, it is not surprising that sexual tensions and temptations would arouse emotions. In Mary Ann's case, she was caught off guard by Jamie's attention. Mary Ann did not know Jamie very well. Later, Mary Ann told me intimate details of their relationship.

After several months, Jamie gained the staff's trust. One afternoon when Mary Ann was in her cell, Jamie approached her. Mary Ann was reading and listening to opera. Jamie entered the entrance to the cell and said, "What a beautiful classical piece of music. Who is that singing?"

Mary Ann looked up at Jamie and responded, "It's Maria Callas, one of the finest opera singers in the world."

Jamie could see that Mary Ann was very interested in classical music, and that classical piano and opera were her favourites. Jamie had picked up a small piece of dark chocolate in the wing and offered it to Mary Ann. She reached out and touched Jamie's hand. Both inmates' eyes locked together. Mary Ann sensed that something happened that day.

The next day, Jamie was cleaning the second floor in front of Mary Ann's cell. She noticed that Jamie was not wearing her baseball cap for the first time. She looked out of her cell and for a minute thought Jamie was a male. Jamie looked into Mary Ann's cell and noticed that she was drawing several buildings. Jamie commented, "What beautiful structures you are drawing."

Mary Ann looked up and responded, "Yes, I enjoy drawing buildings and one day I hope to study architecture." Jamie appeared truly interested in Mary Ann's paintings and drawing and her music.

Mary Ann enjoyed her conversations with Jamie. One day, while staff were busy on the segregation side, Mary Ann confided in Jamie. She asked Jamie what she was doing time for.

Jamie looked up and stared at her. She commented, "I robbed a bank to obtain money for drugs." Jamie thought about it and, after pausing for several seconds, she decided to ask Mary Ann if she felt comfortable talking about her offence. Jamie knew Mary Ann must have committed an offence against children. Somehow Mary Ann trusted Jamie. She quietly said that she was doing a life sentence for stealing a baby from a hospital. Jamie accepted her story.

One Friday afternoon, Jamie was cleaning the lower level. She looked up and noticed Mary Ann looking down at her. Jamie later walked up to clean the second-tier floor in front of Mary Ann's cell. She quickly slipped into Mary Ann's cell and handed her several pictures of well-known limestone buildings in Kingston. Their hands touched. Mary Ann felt something. Her hormones rushed to her head. She enjoyed the touch of another warm human being. Mary Ann remarked that the feeling of another person close by was a real high for her.

Jamie was a long-time lesbian and knew all the techniques and approaches to win over a new female. One Monday morning, she deliberately spent time with another PC inmate in her cell. She sensed that Mary Ann would get a little jealous if this continued. After fifteen minutes, Jamie went upstairs and appeared to be cleaning the range floor. She made a point of not entering Mary Ann's cell. She quickly cleaned the area and went back downstairs.

The next few days, Jamie was ill, and an Asian inmate cleaner entered the PC area. A staff member shadowed her. When the cleaner was in front of Mary Ann's cell, Mary Ann asked where Jamie was. The Asian cleaner responded by telling her that Jamie had been taken to an outside hospital. Mary Ann was concerned. She wanted more information. The Asian inmate had no other details. Mary Ann asked the staff member and was told that no one knew why Jamie was not working that day.

Four days later, Jamie entered the PC area. She worked, cleaning the downstairs floor. Mary Ann recognized her voice. She changed her clothes and put on a more revealing shirt. She undid three buttons. She sprinkled perfume on her neck and chest. Jamie made her way upstairs and heard the music in Mary Ann's cell. Jamie entered Mary Ann's cell and quietly said, "I have missed you."

Jamie gave her a jewellery piece, a little house on a gold chain.

Mary Ann expressed appreciation. She leaned over and kissed Jamie on the check. Jamie responded and put her lips squarely on Mary Ann's lips. She wanted more. Mary Ann grabbed Jamie and kissed her firmly on the lips. Both inmates were excited. Jamie reached over and put her hand on Mary Ann's breast. Their hearts were beating hard. Blood rushed over every part of their bodies. Mary Ann allowed Jamie to reach under her blouse and touch her firm breasts. She wanted more.

It was time for Jamie to return to the landing. The guard was making rounds. Jamie did not want the staff to find her in Mary Ann's room. It was prohibited. Jamie kissed Mary Ann and went to clean the end of the second-floor corridor. Mary Ann was completely sexually aroused. She closed her cell door and moved the shams (curtains) across the entrance to give her some privacy. She couldn't help herself. It was the first time in nearly six years that another person had touched her body. She undressed and masturbated while listening to Beethoven's "Moonlight Sonata."

The next morning, Jamie entered the PC area. It was bath time, and one inmate was in the bath cell. One guard was present in the bottom tier cell completing paperwork. The other guard was handing out cigarettes and lighting them. Jamie cleaned near the guard's office. Mary Ann heard Jamie's voice. She changed into a light-coloured, loosely fitted skirt. She removed her panties and also removed her brassiere.

Jamie made her move when the telephone rang and occupied the guard's attention. This particular guard loved to talk on the telephone. Jamie quickly climbed the stairs with the broom. Mary Ann was the only inmate on the second floor. The other inmate that occupied a cell close to Mary Ann's cell was in the bathtub downstairs. Jamie walked into Mary Ann's cell. She smelled the perfume. She sat down on the bed close to Mary Ann and then kissed her. Mary Ann told me later that their tongues tangled like two snakes preparing a dance of love. They kissed long and passionately. The sexual encounter lasted only three minutes. Jamie had wanted to remove Mary Ann's clothes. Mary Ann told Jamie to wait until Friday morning when the second guard went to get the mail. Before leaving Mary Ann's cell, Jamie whispered to Mary Ann, "I wish I could be with you full time." Jamie left the cell. She was red in the face. Blood had circulated throughout her body and caused a reddish glow.

On Friday morning, Jamie entered the PC area. Mary Ann was receptive to what Jamie had in mind. At 9:45 a.m., the second guard left the area to get the mail. The second inmate living upstairs went to have her tooth pulled by the dentist. The second guard was patrolling the segregation area. The timing was perfect. Jamie took her broom and dustpan and started cleaning. Mary Ann's heard Jamie's voice. She removed her clothes. She washed herself and brushed her teeth. She sprinkled perfume over her body. She played a piano concerto quietly and lay down on the bed. Jamie entered and saw her prize. She kissed Mary Ann and they made love. Then Jamie kissed Mary Ann three or four times and said that she wanted her to think about coming to live in the wing area. Jamie left the cell and continued cleaning the PC area. Within one minute, the bell rang. The second guard entered the unit with the mail.

During the afternoon, I entered the PC segregation area. I made a point of seeing each inmate. Everything was normal this day. There were no problems. When I reached Mary Ann's cell, she spoke very quietly. "Warden Caron, I hope to receive day parole within six months and plan to attend St Lawrence College. I would like to try to live in the wing area.

"It's risky, but I have been here for five years and I need a change. I have gained a friendship with Jamie. She lives in the North Wing and would provide me some security. It's time for me to enter the population."

I was completely surprised. I read the security log books daily and there were no entries or mention of Jamie and Mary Ann being together. I realized that Mary Ann probably would not get out of PC until her full parole. I responded cautiously, "I will check with security staff and speak with the chairperson of the Inmate Committee to see if there are any problems."

Mary Ann reached over and held my hand. "Thank you, Warden. I will accept your decision. I thank you."

The same afternoon, I checked with the AW Security and the Institutional Preventive Security Officer. There were no identified problems. Jamie was known as a lesbian but presented no problems to staff. I discussed the matter with the chairperson of the

Inmate Committee. I asked her to check over the weekend to see if Mary Ann would have any problems due to the proposed move. In addition, I also checked with another strong, informal inmate leader who lived in the wing area and was respected by the population. She was not aware of Mary Ann's background, but gave assurances that her move to the wing would not be problematic.

I was mildly surprised. On Monday, I spoke with the chairperson of the IC. She advised that Mary Ann keep a low profile and not discuss her background with any of the other inmates. She said the committee had no serious concerns. Security staff were also supportive, but had one concern. If Jamie's ex-girlfriend Rita returned to the institution, it would be prudent to review Mary Ann's placement in the wing. It was unlikely Rita would be returning, since she had been transferred to a prison in British Columbia.

It was Mary Ann's time. Monday afternoon, I entered the PC area. Mary Ann was tutoring several PC inmates. I called Mary Ann to come over to the segregation office cell while the officers were in segregation area. She asked, "Do you have a decision for me?"

I quietly answered, "Yes, but it will take another four weeks until a vacant room is available in the North Wing."

Mary Ann smiled and reached out to grab my hand to tell me she appreciated my support. A small tear fell to the floor. "I will do my best to fit in with the population and bring no attention to myself."

I left the PC area with a smile on my face.

Hiking Adventure

During my years at the PFW, there were times when good intentions for program activities proved to be problematic, and, in some cases, disastrous. In 1978, I alternated as acting warden with another manager who was the AW Security. One summer day, the program staff members suggested we take some inmates for a long hike in a wooded parkland that surrounded a lake with cool water. Twelve inmates were screened and approved for escorted temporary absences to an isolated nature preserve.

On Friday morning, we headed out for the park. There were twelve inmates and six staff members, including the acting warden and myself as AW Inmate Programs. The AW Security was acting warden and assumed full responsibility for the outing. Out of the twelve inmates, at least three were marginal and presented some security concerns that required close supervision.

We arrived at the park at 10:15 a.m. The temperature was eighty degrees F. and was expected to climb to eighty-five. About twelve-thirty p.m., the group stopped under a large stand of evergreen trees that provided some cool shade from the hot sun. We all enjoyed the prepared box lunches. At 1:30 p.m., we headed back on the trail towards the hidden lake. The group walked in single file, passing no hikers on the trail. As the temperature increased, the perspiration on each hiker rolled off like a dripping tap in a low-rise rental. As we got closer to the lake, the lead hikers started to hear the rushing of a small stream as it made its way to the lake.

Several of the female hikers were lesbians and enjoyed female company. Unknown to the six staff members, six inmates had planned to run to the lake and jump in before the majority of the group could reach them. I was near the rear of the group. The staff escorts included three males and three female members. The sound of rushing water in the small stream was too much for the six inmates to bear. They ran as hard as they could down the path. The staff at the rear of the group did not know something was happening. The six inmates, who ranged from twenty to forty-three years of age, ran to the lake. They threw off all their clothes and jumped into the lake. When the three male staff members reached the lake, the six naked female inmates were about twenty feet from the shore. They were told to exit the lake and put their clothes back on. The six inmates went around some bushes and put their clothes on. When we returned to the PFW, no one mentioned the day's adventure. On Monday morning, the warden asked me and the AW Security how things went. We said it had been a good day, but we'd had a problem with six inmates who had stripped naked away from the group and jumped into the cool lake.

Two weeks later, the warden was called to his boss's office at Regional Headquarters. Somehow, one of the six inmates had brought a small Polaroid camera and had taken pictures of the five naked inmates. The pictures turned out okay and clearly identified the five inmates. One of the female staff who did not like the AW Security found the pictures in an inmate's cell. She put them in a letter and sent them to the Commissioner of the Canadian Penitentiary Service.

Although we'd had a beautiful day, the AW Security was suspended for two days. I received a written reprimand, and the other staff were given verbal warnings. Although the activity was well planned and received favourable attention, no one thought that our inmates would strip naked. Fortunately, the pictures did not reach the press or other media.

Given the opportunity, some inmates would disrupt a program activity to benefit themselves for their own satisfaction. As far as I was aware, no future escorted temporary absences were arranged to take inmates for a hike, and there were other activities that were cancelled because of an inmate's inappropriate actions. It is unfortunate that a few inmates' actions would ruin a positive activity.

Native Inmates

In 1985, the PFW was almost full. We had 135 inmates in the prison. Segregation was full, and two inmates were in the Institutional Health Care Centre. We had only two vacant cells. There were forty-nine inmates that identified themselves as Aboriginal or Metis (mixed race, Cree and French). The majority of Native inmates came from the four Western provinces of British Columbia, Alberta, Saskatchewan, and Manitoba. There were also three or four Native inmates from the Eastern provinces of New Brunswick and Nova Scotia. The majority of Native inmates came from communities with very poor living conditions. They lacked education and employment work histories. Most of the Native inmates resided in the poor neighbourhoods of the larger urban cities across Canada. Few Native inmates committed offences on their own reserve.

This group presented unique problems for an administrator. The majority of Native inmates received few visits, because their families lived many hundreds—even thousands—of miles away.

It was unfortunate, but many Native inmates did not fully understand or live the way of their Aboriginal heritage. One benefit of serving a federal sentence was that an inmate could learn from the Native Elders that came to the prison.

During the eighties, the inmates had a very strong group called the Native Sisterhood. Elders from Northern Ontario would come to the institution and visit the sisterhood meetings. During the years, the sisterhood received authority from me to conduct powwows. Native foods, dancing, costumes, and drumming were experienced by all. I personally enjoyed the powwows. I always brought my family and three chosen Aboriginal children to share this experience.

During the latter part of the eighties, Native inmates in male institutions and at the Prison for Women were allowed to construct Aboriginal outdoor lodges on the grounds to be used for sweat lodge ceremonies. Inmates under the guidance of female elders would help to prepare the fire and provide the refuge and appropriate conditions for a spiritual, mental, and physical healing.

I recall one year an inmate from a small fishing village on Vancouver Island received two cases of canned salmon. I was asked to allow the food into the prison. Because there was the possibility of inmates' receiving drugs in the cans, it was usually not approved. I could not approve this inmate's request to receive forty-eight cans of salmon. I did allow the inmate, named Marlene, to receive six cans during Sisterhood meetings. The inmate did not violate the security of the institution, and she and members of the Sisterhood were pleased with the compromise. The Native inmates at the prison presented a real challenge because they were from different tribes and reserves across Canada and the USA. Regardless of their background, they all enjoyed the powwows, the Aboriginal drumming, and the cornbread.

I got along with most Native inmates, but there were several inmates that hated all forms of authority. They were difficult to reach. They were very violent and easily set off. I experienced one situation where my life and other people's lives were put at risk.

One day in 1981 when I was making the rounds, I entered the inmate sewing room. A very large Aboriginal inmate from

Canada was extremely upset. She was parading throughout the sewing room with a very large pair of scissors—about eighteen inches long and very sharp. She threatened the older female staff member who was in charge of the sewing room. The sewing room instructor, Mrs. Blackwell, was very upset and afraid to move. She did not say a word. The six other inmates in the sewing room were very fearful. At first I did not understand the issue. I realized that Brenda was extremely upset. Her dark black eyes rolled into her head. She scared me no end.

I listened carefully as I moved closer to Brenda. She kept on complaining that she never received a visit because her family was not approved. Brenda had killed her sister-in-law. This was her second manslaughter conviction. I got two feet from Brenda. She went berserk. She was swinging the sharp scissors around and around in a circular motion. Initially, I believed that she was going to stab someone that day. I sensed that Brenda was close to a nervous breakdown. I quickly summed up the situation. I walked to Brenda and stood in front of her. She ranted and waved the scissors in the air and began to yell uncontrollably. I listened to Brenda for thirty minutes. No one in the room dared to move. I was totally convinced someone would be killed that day.

About forty-five minutes later, I asked Brenda if she wanted anything. She said, "Caron, I want a visit from my family."

I said softly, "If you give me the scissors, I will approve a visit from your family." I continued with the same line for twenty minutes more. Finally, after more than an hour, she appeared to be conciliatory. I said that if she gave me the scissors and went to segregation, no charges would be laid.

Brenda turned around and put the scissors right in front of my eyes. She declared, "Caron, if you approve my family to visit I will gave you the scissors."

I answered, "It's a deal."

Brenda gave me the scissors and walked to segregation under escort. Brenda, who was near the end of her sentence in sixty days, was nervous. This was common for some inmates who are unprepared to return to the community. Brenda could not handle the realization that she would be released on Mandatory Supervision in a short time. She was released from segregation within four days. Her family never came to visit. Brenda was released on MS and travelled out West. She was killed in a knife fight one year later.

In all my years in the prison, this was the event in which I felt the most concern for my safety, as well as the safety of other people in the sewing room. Brenda had killed two people before and could easily have killed again. I earned my salary that day. In this case I was lucky.

After the incident was over, two inmates approached me and thanked me for my intervention. The two young inmates cried and said that they had thought they would be killed. A third inmate who had been in the sewing room stopped me in the hall and said that I had handled Brenda with sensitivity. She said that my intervention defused a potentially lethal situation. This black inmate told me that she bad-mouthed me before, but after today she realized that I knew my job. Before leaving our encounter, she commented that she would not be returning to the prison. She said, "I have had enough shit today to last a lifetime." She hugged me and returned to her living area.

When I arrived home after work, my wife asked me how was my day. I replied, "I was very stressed. I need a glass of wine."

Mary Ann's Move to the Population

Mary Ann was moved to the North Wing area of the prison six weeks later. She was assigned a room that was three rooms away from Jamie's. It was difficult for Mary Ann to leave the security of the PC area. Her fellow PC inmates wished her well. Mary Ann's move to the wing was an inspiration for another young inmate named Joy, who was in PC for having sex with an eleven-year-old boy. Joy waited until early December to make the move. Although there were positive signs that she could live in the wing without problems, Joy had no security blanket like Jamie to help with her transition. It was a bold step for a PC inmate to enter the population. Joy's move was uneventful. She lived in the wing for six weeks, at which time her status changed. An inmate from her hometown was admitted to the institution. It was unfortunate that the new inmate was a close friend of the mother of the eleven-year-old victim. The new inmate, along with another tough inmate, cornered Joy in the gym one night and said that she would cut her face for sexually abusing her friend's young son. Joy felt very uncomfortable and asked security staff to return her to the PC area.

Mary Ann's move to the wing was not without problems. After three days, two French inmates from Quebec approached her in the washroom one night and said that they didn't like people that took advantage of children. They believed incorrectly that Mary Ann had killed a small child. They made it known that they would get her at their first opportunity. A guard walked into the washroom and Mary Ann returned to her room. A few minutes later, Jamie entered Mary Ann's room. She could tell that Mary Ann was upset and had tears in her eyes. Mary Ann told her that the two French inmates from the South Wing approached her in the washroom and made threatening remarks about her possible background. She described the two inmates. The next morning at breakfast, Mary Ann pointed out the inmates who had approached her. Later that day, Jamie found them alone in the poolroom. Jamie walked up to the two young inmates with her fist clenched. She slugged the larger French inmate on the side of her face. The strong blow knocked the inmate down. Jamie shouted, "Listen, Frenchy, if you and your fucking friend speak to or touch my friend Mary Ann because of her background again you will go home in a body bag. Do you bitches understand?"

The young French inmate said, "We are sorry. We were told that Mouse had killed a child."

Jamie sharply responded, "Mouse did not hurt any child."

The two French inmates retreated after telling Jamie they would leave Mouse alone. Jamie did not tell her about this incident until she was granted day parole.

Mary Ann experienced no problems after this. Jamie made it known to the population that Mary Ann was her "girl." She always escorted her to the kitchen and dining room. In addition, Jamie escorted Mary Ann each day to the Health Care Centre to pick up her medicine. Mary Ann was happy to be out of the PC Unit. She truly enjoyed her freedom. She attended school every day. In early

May, Mary Ann received a letter from the National Parole Board stating that she would have a hearing in mid-June to decide if she would be granted escorted temporary and day parole.

6

The Video Program

As previously mentioned, one of the best program activities that we have to offer inmates are visits. Unfortunately, many inmates are admitted to the prison from across Canada and other countries around the world. In order to improve inmate contact with family, I started a new program that gained international attention.

In 1982, approximately fifty percent of the population was from other provinces and countries, including the USA. One day, I got an idea for a positive new program. If an inmate serving a long sentence from a distant province made a videotape, we could arrange to send it to her loved one or family member and have the tape viewed.

I needed a community group to help me. I approached a local service club (Knights of Columbus) that had councils in other provinces and states. I spoke to the local club executive one night. I told them that if an inmate completed a tape, we would like to send it to another city where another council of their organization would be present. The council in the other city would receive the tape and take it to the family to view. In addition, they would tape the family's own love letter and presentation and send a completed videotape back to the prison for the inmate's viewing. I was encouraged when a local council of the Knights of Columbus agreed to participate in the project. I ran the program proposal by the program committee. Chaplain Bill, an energetic Baptist minister who was willing to help out wherever he could, agreed to be the contact person for the program.

I approved the expenditure for thirty videotapes and a new VCR television system to record and review finished tapes. Reverend Bill was very eager to get this program off the ground. The first inmate that participated was a lifer in her late twenties. She had a young daughter who resided out West. Jennifer prepared a beautiful tape of her reading children's books and playing the guitar and singing her favourite songs. It was so exciting to see Jennifer reach out to her young daughter, who was being cared for by her grandmother.

The first completed tape and a blank tape were sent out in early June. The Knights of Columbus in Vancouver received the tapes within seven days. Jennifer's daughter and her mother viewed the tape and prepared their own taped message. The first tape received was from Jennifer's mother and daughter and it arrived two weeks later. I remember the day the first tape arrived. After receiving Jennifer's first tape, Reverend Bill called me and set up a meeting with Jennifer to review the tape at three p.m. Jennifer invited me to review the tape after she first watched it. Jennifer was excited, anxious, and thrilled to see the tape of her daughter and mother. She reminded me of a small child opening her first Christmas gift. It was a beautiful sight to see Jennifer reviewing intensely the video images of her young daughter. Several other inmates participated in the program.

In early December, Jennifer agreed to have a national newspaper reporter from Toronto come to the prison and interview her, Reverend Bill, and myself. The reporter was very sensitive to Jennifer's concerns. The reporter told Jennifer that she would not mention her daughter's name in the newspaper. It was a well-written newspaper article that included a picture of Jennifer preparing a Christmas message for her daughter. The newspaper article was well received in the population.

I received a telephone call from a television executive from NBC's *Good Morning America* program wanting to do an interview. I was flattered by the attention, but I declined the interview. Four weeks later, Jennifer received a disturbing telephone call from her mother. The Toronto newspaper article had been copied and used by an unscrupulous editor in a sister newspaper in Vancouver as part of the national chain. This time the newspaper ran Jennifer's story showing her preparing a Christmas message for her daughter. Adjacent to this article was an article and picture of the male victim that Jennifer was convicted of murdering. This article showed a picture of the victim's widow putting flowers on her husband's grave at Christmastime. Although the

Toronto newspaper writer had agreed to respect Jennifer's confidential concerns, the newspaper editor in Vancouver decided to ignore this concern and champion the male victim's story.

This was probably the most horrendous dishonest media portrayal against an unsuspecting inmate that I have ever encountered. I clearly remember Jennifer asking me if it would be okay to be interviewed by the Toronto newspaper. I told her that the reporter advised me that she would honour and respect Jennifer's privacy. I was so angry, I refused newspaper interviews for three years. The video program continued for several more years. Later, Jennifer worked as a program coordinator under Reverend Bill's supervision and helped other inmates prepare videotapes for their families.

The Braille program

Given the long period of time that some PC inmates had to endure, I was always looking for program opportunities to occupy the small group in a relatively limited space. Inmates could take correspondence courses or tutor other students. One day in 1979, I was fortunate to meet the executive director of the local Canadian National Institute of the Blind (CNIB), which was located at the end of our parking lot. After a lengthy conversation during the lunch hour, the executive director invited me to his office. He mentioned that he was looking for volunteers to transcribe books into Braille. I told Mr. Brown that I had a small group of women that might be interested in the project. Mr. Brown, who was non-sighted, said that he would like to talk to the inmates.

Later that day, I went to the PC unit and asked the inmates how many of them would be interested in the Braille program. To my surprise, five out of the seven inmates agreed to meet with Mr. Brown. I telephoned Mr. Brown and made an appointment for the next day at 1:30 p.m. Mr. Brown entered the prison with one Braille transcriber machine and some Braille paper. I escorted him to the PC area of the prison. He was an engaging individual who had the gift of talking to people. He made the inmates feel comfortable. He explained that there were seventy-five people in the Kingston community who required Braille books.

The inmates listened with interest. He told the group that it would take about two to three weeks to complete a book, depending on the size of the book and how many hours a person worked on the assignment. After hearing Mr. Brown's presentation, three inmates signed up for the program to transcribe English books onto Braille paper. The following week, Mr. Brown brought over three transcriber machines and three boxes of Braille paper. I arranged for the three inmates who participated in the Braille program to be compensated as if they were in the school program.

At the end of the first month, three books were completely transcribed into Braille. The task of transcribing books into Braille is a time-demanding activity. The inmates worked on the book for two hours in the morning and two hours in the afternoon. If an inmate wanted to work more hours, she could work in her cell at night. It was necessary that they pace themselves and not become bored with this repetitious task.

After three months, only two inmates had the staying power and desire to continue with the program. The inmates received a beautiful thank-you letter from a sightless recipient.

I remembered one day when Mr. Brown telephoned and said he had a request from a non-sighted seventeen-year-old girl who needed her Grade 12 high school books transcribed into Braille. The two inmates agreed to work on this project. The Braille program lasted for approximately three years. At the end of the third year, four inmates were transcribing books into Braille. The CNIB found a new electronic method to transcribe books into Braille.

The inmates who participated in this program gained a lot of personal satisfaction when the jobs were completed. The letter of appreciation from the seventeen-year-old non-sighted girl brought tears to the participants' eyes. They all realized that the program had merit. Each Christmas, Mr. Brown arranged for a large basket of fruit and chocolate to be delivered to the prison for the benefit of the inmates who had participated in the Braille program.

Mary Ann's National Parole Board Experience

One day in early June, I was making my rounds of the institution. That day I started by visiting the Health Care Centre. I entered the nursing station and talked briefly with the duty nurse and Mrs. Thomas, the Chief of Health Care. The institution was fortunate to have registered nurses working around the clock at the prison. The nurses have to have various skills to work in a prison environment. A good, effective nurse has emergency room skills, knowledge of pediatrics, geriatrics, psychology, and medications, and post-operative know-how. A successful nurse will also have good listening skills, common sense, and a good sense of humour. Mrs. Thomas had attracted an excellent team of dedicated and hard-working nurses.

Mrs. Thomas told me that she had three overnight patients in the hospital rooms. Two inmates were recovering from surgery that had been performed at the community hospital. When I entered the quiet room, I was surprise to see Mary Ann as a patient. I said, "How are you today?"

She looked up with sad eyes and uttered a few words. "Mr. Caron, I am so stressed that I cannot sleep. I haven't eaten in two days."

I looked at her and responded, "What's happening?"

She answered, "My Parole Board hearing is on Friday and I am concerned about leaving Jamie behind. I am so nervous about my hearing. I looked at Willy's case. Last month, Willy walked into the Parole Board hearing and after thirty minutes was denied. Furthermore, they told her that she should not apply again for two years." Mary Ann started to cry like a baby. "I can't do any more time. I worry about Jamie and what will happen to our relationship."

I stood up from the chair and firmly directed my comments at Mary Ann's inner self. "Listen, Mouse, you have a life to live. First of all, Jamie helped you to get this far. You have made tremendous progress. Jamie cares for you and wants you to move ahead. By the way, Jamie has had three girlfriends over the years at the prison and you will not be the last. Jamie has acted as your jumper cables. She has started your motor. The rest is up to you. In terms of your parole application, you have excellent reports with positive support from a variety of staff. As for myself, I have recommended that you receive escorted TA's to prepare for your college entrance. I feel confident that the Parole Board members will look favourably at your application. I suggest you start eating and go back to the wing and spend some time with Jamie. She needs you to be strong."

Mary Ann sat up in her bed and said, "Thank you, Mr. Caron. I needed that. Your words have helped me." Mary Ann shook my hand as I started to leave the room. Mary Ann checked out of hospital two hours later, after eating some soup and crackers.

On Friday, Mary Ann put on her best clothes and proceeded to the chapel to meet the Parole Board members. With Jamie, she had rehearsed her responses to a variety of possible questions. Mary Ann told me later that she first went into a side office and kneeled down and prayed to God to give her a positive outcome.

Mary Ann was the first inmate to appear before the Parole Board that day. Outside the hearing room, Jamie waited like an expectant parent with six other inmate friends who had their fingers and toes crossed. There were three board members, two middle-aged women and one older man. Mary Ann recalled that they had asked her many questions, some of which she had rehearsed. She openly admitted her guilt and reported that she had written the baby's parents five years ago asking them for their forgiveness. She told the board members that her action was wrong and ill-conceived. Mary Ann spoke positively about her school studies and her desire to attend St Lawrence College and to enroll in the architecture technologist two-year program. Mary Ann told the Board that she had been accepted into the program.

Two other inmates appeared before the National Parole Board that day. Mary Ann walked out with a large smile across her face. She had tears in her eyes, but they were tears of joy. She looked at Jamie and said, "I got it." They embraced. Mary Ann explained that she would receive escorted TA's until her day parole started in early September. She would return nightly for one month, and then she would be released to the Elizabeth Fry Society's halfway house. All three board members voted in favour of Mary Ann's parole application. The other two inmates that saw the Parole Board that day were not successful; their parole applications were denied.

Before the day was over, Mary Ann asked to see me. She walked into my office and noticed the painting on the wall that she had given me several years before. She said, "Thank you, Mr. Caron, for your ongoing support." Mary Ann told me that my words early this week had given her confidence and had helped to put her priorities in order. She left my office a new woman. She was full of confidence and willing to tackle life's experiences head-on. Her journey continued.

Portrait of the author.
(Courtesy Mary Ann)

Transsexual Inmates (Gender Dysphoria)

During my tenure as warden, I encountered many different situations, and people of every background. There was one area that I knew nothing about. I had to do some homework to understand the dynamic of these inmates. One day, during mid-morning when I was making my institutional tour, I entered "A" range, the largest range in the prison, where the most difficult inmates resided along with other inmates that were "different."

When I passed Cell 11, a voice from inside called out. It was Shirley, a thirty-three-year-old white inmate who was serving life for murder. Shirley was a transsexual. Transsexuals are persons born as one sex, but physically trapped in a body of the opposite sex. After a sex-change operation and continuous hormone therapy, they are changed into the form of the opposite sex. As I got close to Shirley's cell, she said quietly, "Warden, any news on my request for special procedure?"

I answered in the negative. "Shirley, as I mentioned before, I do not believe the service will pay for the special procedures that you have requested. To be honest with you, I am not aware of our service approving additional medical procedures. Your request has been sent to Regional Headquarters and after their review and comments, your request will be sent to National Headquarters. I don't believe you will get a decision for two months."

Shirley looked up and said two words: "Thanks, Warden."

"By the way, Shirley, that is a lovely picture of a horse that you are drawing."

"Thank you." Shirley was from out West and loved horses.

There were three transsexual inmates in the prison when I was warden. Shirley was originally serving a life sentence as a man in a maximum security prison in British Columbia. She had requested and received authorization from our service to pay for the specialized surgery at the university hospital. In Shirley's case, the male sex organs were surgically removed and hormone therapy was started. No person with male genitals would be admitted to the Prison for Women.

Shirley had requested that two additional medical procedures be approved by the service. She wanted to have a breast augmentation procedure as well as have her vagina enlarged. The other two transsexual inmates had had their medical procedures completed before they came to prison. They did not request additional medical procedures. I was not aware that our service would pay for any more transsexual surgery.

I found that generally the transsexual inmates were different in that they had larger and more muscular bodies, larger hands, larger noses, and deeper and stronger voices. The transsexual inmates did not pose serious management problems. They all had their own personalities and blended well into the population. On family days, the transsexual inmates loved to dress up as women and were not out of place in the population. I personally accepted each transsexual inmate as a woman who had unique personal needs. I never encountered a female inmate who wanted to be a male. There were a dozen or more aggressive homosexual women who had a very muscular presentation but did not apply for a procedure to change their sex.

Inmates That "Didn't Belong"

Near the end of the "A" range, I encountered four misplaced inmates who really stood out from the others. They were all from New Brunswick and Newfoundland. They were definitely slower than other members in the population.

I remember one of them, named Mabel. She was a thirty-three-year-old Native woman who was always friendly and loved to talk to the staff. Mabel grew up on a reserve and was proud of her Native background. She had a harelip and slurred her words. Sometimes when she was anxious it was difficult to understand what she was saying. She walked with a sight limp. Mabel occupied the fourth-last cell on Lower "A" range. When I approached Mabel's cell, I always received the same question: "Hello, Warden. Do you have a cigarette?" Every time I saw Mabel, she would ask me for a smoke. Then, "Will you give me a pass so I can go downtown and buy some candy?"

I responded, "Mabel, you know that you are not eligible for eight months. Please ask me in April."

Mabel was serving her second federal sentence of three years and ten months for breaking into a church to keep warm during a cold winter night. I reviewed Mabel's lengthy criminal record and observed that with the exception of one break and enter conviction, Mabel's record had a history of nuisance offences. Mabel loved to press fire alarms and watch the fire trucks speed off to a location. Mabel and the other three inmates at the end of the range had similar offences. The provincial correctional authority's hands were tied. They were closing mental hospital beds, and jail cells were full. It was a real shame, but in my opinion all four inmates at the end of Lower "A" range did not belong in prison. All four women were friendly and always talked to the staff. Hardened inmates ignored them. Sometimes they made fools of them. Probably the main reason why tough criminally minded inmates did not like them was because they talked to the guards and periodically revealed more sensitive, revealing information than certain inmates would like.

The inmate that I really was fond of was Betty, a thirty-eight-year-old grossly heavy-set woman serving four years for breaking into and entering a liquor store. Betty had low intelligence and was easily taken advantage of. She loved to play poker, but never won a single game. She always lost her weekly small wage to other inmates. Every time I saw Betty, she would ask me for a smoke.

It was so sad to see these four inmates in the prison. In reality, these four inmates probably received better care in terms of food, medical attention, and clothing than they would on the streets of their hometowns. Betty was a three-time loser. I asked her what brought her back this time.

"Warden, I needed my teeth fixed and I did not have any money, so I threw a large stone through the Hudson's Bay store window and stole a teddy bear off Santa's sleigh."

I vividly remember Betty's last release from the prison. Betty was released on Mandatory Supervision and was to live at the Elizabeth Fry halfway house for six weeks. One night I received a telephone call from the Duty Correctional Supervisor at three a.m. She said that Betty had pounded on the front door with her fists wanting back into the prison. She was crying and upset because she missed her friends at the end of the range. The Duty Correctional Supervisor did not have the authority to admit any inmate at night. It was very unusual and not an accepted practice to receive inmates directly from the street. In this case, I approved Betty's request and told the supervisor to place her in the hospital until we could sort out her problems in the morning. I suggested the supervisor telephone the night supervisor at the Elizabeth Fry Society's halfway house and advise them that we had Betty in custody.

I was very appreciative of my staff's attention to these four inmates. The matrons treated the four inmates like children and helped them cope with the reality of prison life. There was one slower inmate named Maggie who entered the prison several years later. Maggie was a thirty-three-year-old white woman who was noticeably overweight. Maggie, who was from New Brunswick, had been admitted to the prison for three assault convictions. Maggie's problem was that she couldn't express herself properly; therefore, she got upset very easily and would strike out by punching her adversaries. Maggie wasn't really dangerous, but she was stubborn like an ox and numerous times refused to listen to directions from the staff. Frequently we had to place her in segregation because she would kick or punch a staff member when she was asked to do something. My guess is that Maggie spent half her time in segregation. The Salvation Army in her hometown completed arrangements for Maggie to be placed on a farm with loving and supportive guardians. Maggie never returned to prison again after her release and placement on the farm.

Necole's Story

Several months passed without any major problems. I would see Mary Ann in the wing area or sometimes in the dining room. I always tried to talk to her away from other inmates in order to protect her from drawing unnecessary heat and questions from negative inmates trying to determine what I had to say. There was a lot of paranoia in the prison. Unfortunately, inmates in prison didn't trust easily, so the facts got distorted and twisted and sometimes the result was serious harm.

I recall a middle-aged woman named Summer who entered the prison on a serious drug conviction. This inmate enjoyed putting out the balls and throwing them any which way. One day, a new inmate named Necole arrived at the prison and was placed on "A" range. This new inmate didn't know what had hit her. Summer spread rumours that Necole was an informer for the horsemen (Royal Canadian Mounted Police) and that she had given evidence that resulted in several women's getting long sentences for drug importation. Summer happened to tell this story to the wrong inmates. Several of these difficult inmates were known enforcers and had no respect for the police and their "rats."

One night, Necole was cornered by three inmates in the backroom of the gymnasium and confronted. Necole told the group she had not been the informer, since at the time she was in provincial lock-up for six months for being intoxicated behind the wheel of a stolen truck. Ignoring this, they pressed on. Finally one inmate pulled out a homemade shiv and stabbed Necole in the chest and neck. She yelled at Necole, "Here is what we do to fucking rats." The other two inmates kicked Necole in the stomach and legs before the three left the gymnasium laughing and acting tough.

The staff found Necole lying in a pool of blood. She was taken by ambulance to the Kingston General Hospital and received emergency surgery. Necole refused to co-operate with the police and identify her assailants. Several months later, a black inmate named Mandy entered the prison. Somehow she heard what had happened to Necole. She backed up Necole's story. She stated that Necole was in the provincial jail during the time she was alleged to have ratted on the drug addicts. Necole found out that it was Summer who had passed on the rumour that she was a rat. One night, Necole caught Summer in the tunnel on the way to the gym. She punched Summer into unconsciousness. She yelled at Summer as she fell to the floor, "I will kill you, bitch, if you ever again lie and tell stories about another person." Necole kicked Summer in the mouth and knocked out three teeth.

Summer awoke within a few seconds and walked up the stairs to the Health Care Centre. She reported to the nurse that she had fallen down the back stairs of the range. Summer suffered no lasting injuries. Her face and arms were stiff from the beating, and she had a black eye. She had to be fitted with a dental prosthesis. I never heard of Summer's ever again speaking negatively about another inmate. She was released on parole the following year and never returned to the prison.

Mary Ann's First Temporary Absence

In early July, I saw Mary Ann one day in the Health Care Centre. She was seeing the institutional physician for her annual medical. Mary Ann was in a good mood. She told me that she was a little nervous, because on Monday she was going on her first escorted temporary absence since she was first arrested in late

1979. We were alone in the waiting room. I asked what she would do for her first pass. She looked up and commented, "Well, first I want to go to the college and see my advisor and pick up some information on my course of study. I then want to have lunch and order something off the menu that I don't get in here." She giggled for a few seconds and said, "I miss having a T-bone steak with jumbo shrimps and baked potato. I love dark chocolate ice cream." I could see Mary Ann was gearing up for her day out. "In addition, I want to get some pictures of unique buildings in the city. Finally, I want to buy something small for Jamie at the S & R department store in downtown Kingston that I see advertised in the local newspaper. The last item I will buy will be a tape of Joan Sutherland's favourite opera arias."

"Who is going to escort you for seven hours?"

"Reverend Bill. He knows the city well and has taken many girls out of the prison on their pass."

"Good luck on your pass. By the way, I have meetings away from the prison on Monday, so I won't be here to see you walk to the parking lot. Enjoy your day out."

On Sunday night, Mary Ann could not get any sleep. She finally awoke at seven a.m., took a shower, and got dressed. She went to breakfast with Jamie. At eight-thirty a.m., Mary Ann went to the classification department and signed some papers for her release. Mary Ann hugged Jamie and gave her a big kiss. Jamie had a small tear in her eye and said, "Go for it, girl. Have a great day." Mary Ann left the institution with Reverend Bill at 9:01 a.m.

Mary Ann arrived back at the institution at four p.m. Jamie was up in the chapel and could see Mary Ann walking up the front sidewalk, returning to the prison. Jamie returned to the wing to wait for Mary Ann's arrival. Jamie cleaned up Mouse's room. She couldn't wait to hear all the news that Mary Ann had to tell. Mary Ann had agreed to pick up two packs of Dentyne gum for her. At four-thirty p.m., Mary Ann made it to her room. She hugged Jamie and went into her room for some privacy and to give her friend a little gift. According to Reverend Bill, Mary Ann had accomplished everything that she wanted on her first pass.

Male Guards

One of the changes that occurred at the prison happened in 1978. At that time, a number of male guards were not performing effectively in male prisons, for a number of reasons. Either they were too passive, indifferent, and/or lacked motivation, or were too aggressive; or were just not effective working with male inmates. The Regional Director of Ontario Region made an offer to my predecessor that he was unable to refuse.

My predecessor fought the transfer of twelve male correctional officers to the Prison for Women. He knew some of the men and had heard about others from other wardens. The introduction of male corrections officers was not necessarily a bad decision, but male correctional officers with no previous training and knowledge of the female offender was problematic. Many of the hardened female offenders had been abused and taken advantage of by males. Some female inmates hated all men.

The male correctional officers were predominantly assigned tasks in the front control centre, sally port area, and escort duties. The male officers also served to inspect the inside yard complex at night and assisted female correctional officers in inmate transfers to other locations. Later, some of the male correctional officers transferred to the outside hospital escort duties.

This move involving male correctional officers caused many problems. First of all, less aggressive female guards would call their male counterparts when physical confrontation and force were necessary. Some of male guards took active roles in subduing aggressive females. Sometimes the mere presence of male correctional officers on the range brought out the worst in some inmates. They taunted some of the male officers and were ready to rumble.

In time, some of the male correctional officers adjusted and were effective working with female offenders. In other cases, some male correctional officers could not manage their new roles and asked for a transfer.

Looking back, I believe I fired only two employees for not performing their required duties. I recall one officer that would vacate his one-person evening post at the sally port and go downtown and pick up a pizza. This action was totally unacceptable.

This male officer was disciplined on several occasions. If a fire had occurred during the guard's absence, or an ambulance had been required because of staff illness or inmate injury, the vehicle could not have entered the compound while the guard was out buying his supper. After the third incident, the male guard was fired as part of progressive discipline. The guard was off many months (eleven months) as he and his union defended his rights at a federal adjudication hearing. In this case, the federal adjudicator ruled that the employee had an alcohol problem and needed treatment. We had to take the employee back but he lost eleven months of his salary. We had to pay for his twelve-week addiction treatment course.

The male employee returned to work, and after four weeks, I had to fire him again. In this instance, the employee opened the main control door to talk to three inmates serving life sentences instead of talking to the inmates through the small hole in the control office Plexiglas window. If the three inmates had rushed the officer and gained control of the front control post, the entire institution would have been at risk. Mass escapes would have been possible. A senior female security officer noticed the male officer's poor judgment. The male officer appealed his termination and used his union's assistance for support. His case was reviewed by a federal court adjudicator within nine weeks. The adjudicator denied the appeal and upheld his termination.

In 1984, I was asked by my boss to provide a tour of the prison for a senior prison administrator responsible for correctional institutions in one of the large states in Australia. During the tour, the official noticed that I had about a dozen males working in the prison. The official from Australia asked if I had any problems with the male guards. I remember telling him that I had some problems with certain male guards because they did not have the right temperament and background to work with female prisoners. The official from Australia laughed and said that was not what he meant. "We have male guards working in some female prisons. In one prison, out of fifteen male guards on staff, eleven were involved in relationships with female correctional officers. It was so bad that some female officers could not work certain shifts in order to avoid a conflict between two female guards fighting over a male guard."

I looked at him and said that we had the same problem here. I stated that I thought nine out of our twelve male guards were involved in relationships with female guards. We had the same problem of trying to find different shifts for certain male and female guards. A number of marital relationships were ended because of a relationship between a male and female guard. It was difficult enough to manage a female prison, but sorting out problems relating to relationships between the staff only made the situation more complex.

Mary Ann's morale improved during July and August. She had four escorted temporary absences and was becoming knowledgeable of the city and its bus routes. She told me that Reverend Bill was very helpful. She took several buses and found her way to the college. One day, Mary Ann visited the Elizabeth Fry Society halfway house and introduced herself to the woman in charge of the house. When she entered the halfway house, she noticed that one of the French inmates who had given her a bad time in the wing area was now residing in the house. Mary Ann didn't speak to her and knew that she might have a problem with this inmate. In two weeks, Mary Ann would be starting her college course. She got to know her advisor and they developed a positive relationship. Mary Ann told me that no one at the college was aware of her background. During her last two outings, Mary Ann picked up several of her textbooks and was reading them at night. She went out one day with her classification officer and bought some new clothes; when she dressed up, she looked like a college student. Each night, Mary Ann dreamed about leaving the prison and starting a new life. She mentioned that leaving Jamie still bothered her. Jamie accepted the reality of their relationship and tried not to say anything that would lead Mouse down a road of depression.

Mother and Daughter Inmates

During the last week of August, the Inmate Sentence Administrator asked to see me. She told me that we were getting three new inmates the next day from the Toronto West Detention Centre and that there must have been a mistake with the names. Two of the inmates had the same first and last names. I commented that it could be a mistake, but checked their admission documents extra closely and made sure they had signed a waiver on infectious diseases.

The next morning at around eleven a.m., a bus arrived at the front of the prison and three handcuffed inmates walked up the front sidewalk towards the front door. I watched the small caravan proceeding around the outside worker and his wheelbarrow. I observed two middle-aged inmates and a young woman in her mid-twenties. The Inmate Sentence Administrator checked the new inmates' documents and when everything was in order, she called for security staff to escort the inmates inside the belly of the prison. It was always a difficult moment for a new inmate to enter the prison, with all its electronic metal gates and loud noises. The Inmate Sentence Administrator approached my secretary and asked to see me.

The Inmate Sentence Administrator told me that we had a mother and daughter entering the prison. I was advised that the two family members were charged with drug trafficking (mules) and sentenced to seven years. Mrs. Marilyn Smith and her daughter Miss Marilyn Jackie Smith were part of a large group of mules who had been arrested and convicted of smuggling narcotics into Canada from South America.

I interviewed both women and found them to be very pleasant. This was the first criminal conviction for both women. The two newcomers, who were Americans, were utterly shocked to have received a seven-year sentence. Both women were assigned to "B" range. The mother told me that they had met a handsome man in South America who had promised them ten thousand dollars each if they would carry the false-bottom suitcases into Canada.

Mrs. Smith and her daughter were the second daughter and mother combination that entered the prison while I was warden. I remember another mother and daughter combination that had been admitted after being found guilty of manslaughter in the death of the mother's common-law husband.

Mrs. Smith and her daughter were not criminally minded. They were short on cash in South America and thought that it would be easy to smuggle cocaine into Canada. They didn't know about Spot, the small terrier that was on police duty at the airport customs office. Little Spot had caught five people in three days carrying drugs into Canada. He had a perfect nose for cocaine.

Mrs. Smith and her daughter fit in well with the thirteen other mules, eight of whom were foreign born, that we had in the institution. They both worked in the sewing room. They presented absolutely no problems to staff. Mrs. Smith told me that there had been nineteen men and women mules arrested, including the alleged kingpin, a businessman from New York. The drug leader was in the Toronto West Detention Centre. He had lots of money and appealed his conviction of drug trafficking and his eighteen-year sentence.

Mrs. Smith and her daughter had spent almost two and a half years of their sentence and were paroled for deportation on their eligibility date to the USA. The male ringleader had spent almost the same amount of time in provincial jail appealing his conviction before being transferred to a male prison in the Kingston area. He was arriving at the male prison to continue his sentence as the two Smith ladies were returning to the USA.

Accreditation

Over the years, the Prison for Women was criticized by various reports as Canada's only female maximum security prison because it was too old, did not have enough programs, and was in great need of modernization. The PFW was also criticized in that it contained maximum-, medium-, and minimum-security inmates under one roof. Given some of the limitations due to the physical plant, I was extremely proud when the institution received a highly desired Accreditation Certificate in 1982 for a three-year term from the American Accreditation Association Standards. The administration was greatly appreciative of the work that all departments completed to receive this designation. I was especially grateful to Ann, the hard-working classification officer who acted as our taskmaster and coordinator of the program. Ann worked long hours and used her organizational skills to achieve the highest results and the prestigious Accreditation Standard designation. In order to obtain the Accreditation Standard, the institution had to change and rewrite a lot of standing orders, policy documents, emergency crisis management documents, medical policies, and personnel and human resource policies; make security upgrades; and develop and implement new programs and activities to reach the high goals set for the Accreditation Standards. I was very proud of our team. Many male institutions as well as the Prison for Women applied for the Accreditation Standard. Not all the male institutions were successful in obtaining the American Accreditation Standard. The final results were a testimony to the co-operative spirit and dedication of all managers and staff that had worked on this daunting task.

One of the things the institution had to do was upgrade the security of our inmate files and security documents. This was especially evident one month when classification staff complained that their files were being moved around their office and desk area. We installed some privacy cameras, and to our surprise found that some inmates who used one of the two television rooms that were located down the hall from the case management offices were seen at night lifting the ceiling panels and climbing up and moving and shimmying their bodies along the ceiling over the case management offices. I gave the inmates credit for using their ingenuity. This breach of security resulted in our cancelling television viewing in the two rooms and changing the ceiling's building materials in the television rooms and in the classification officers' offices.

7

Mary Ann's Final Days at the Prison for Women

It was early September 1985. In four days, Mary Ann would be walking out of the institution on her own steam. She would have no one to hold her hand or drive her to where she wanted to go. That day, Mary Ann told me that she was happy to start her new adventure on conditional day parole[21] and walk the streets as a free bird. Mary Ann was well organized. In her room she had all her school books and materials on her desk. She had only two pictures on her walls. Both pictures were of two of her favourite buildings. Jamie's picture was on her dresser. Mary Ann told me that she and Jamie were ready for that day. She remarked that Jamie was more prepared and understanding of the situation. Mary Ann quietly mentioned to me that she had deliberately played down her achievements and attendance at college. Inside, Mouse was gradually getting the strength to wean herself from Jamie's positive support.

On the first day of college, Mary Ann was up early and showered. She put on her new clothes and grabbed her purse and shoulder bag, which contained her lunch, school books, and writing materials. She hugged Jamie and kissed her in her room. Jamie looked at Mouse and said, "Go for it, girl. Good luck. I love you." This time Jamie had a small tear in the corner of her eye. It was not easy for her. Even though this was the fourth time that she'd had to get used to someone she cared about leaving, it nevertheless was difficult. Jamie gave Mouse a little ring to remind her of their friendship.

Mary Ann passed through the front gate at 8:15 a.m. She walked about twenty feet and turned back. She rushed to the

---

21 For one month, she would have to return to the prison each afternoon and spend the night there.

front door and pressed the button. The female correctional officer who was at in the front control yelled out at Mary Ann, "Have you changed your mind?"

Mary Ann quickly replied, "No, I forgot my day parole certificate. Please call the wing. Jamie can get it and bring it to me. It's on my dresser. Thank you." The officer called down to the wing. Within four minutes, Jamie appeared at the second barrier and handed the certificate to her. Mary Ann exited the institution after thanking Jamie.

I watched as Mary Ann walked away, full of the confidence and determination she had received as gifts. She walked towards the bus stop located nearby. She was on her way. Mary Ann got on the bus and arrived at the college in twenty-five minutes.

Mary Ann was released on day parole each day during the week to attend college. She would remain at the prison until the end of September. I watched her leave in the morning and sometimes I watched her return close to four-thirty p.m. Each day she seemed to gain more momentum and self-confidence. The greatest joy I received as a warden was seeing an inmate like Mary Ann expand her horizon and gradually regain her spirit and place in the world.

Linda, the Wheeler-Dealer

Sometimes an inmate who was cunning and had special skills, if given the right opportunity, would seize the moment and advance her fortunes at the expense of others. I recall an inmate named Linda, a forty-two-year-old Jewish woman, who was very bright but possessed a criminal mind and desired to obtain riches by fraudulent means. Linda was slightly overweight, but covered her expanding waistline with expensive, oversized clothing. Linda was serving four years for fraud. She had a history of fraud convictions stretching over fifteen years. Linda had the gift of gab. She could sell sand to countries with large tracts of deserts in their borders. She was convincing and lethal at the same time.

Following Linda's admission to the prison, she applied for a job as a clerk for Nancy, the Chief of Social Development. Nancy had a friendly way about her. She was engaging and enjoyed activities to the beat of her own drum. She had flair and excitement about her being. She was a gamer who sought out new adventures. She attended many meetings and events and had a difficult time managing the small, trivial activities and events in her department. At the work board, I expressed some concerns and arguments against placing Linda as a clerk in the Social Development Department. However, Nancy was drowning in paperwork and needed an organized person to help run her department. The slim majority felt sorry for Nancy and recommended that Linda work for her. Given that there were no other candidates and that Nancy wanted Linda to work for her, the work assignment was approved.

Initially, Linda did an excellent job for Nancy. She had all Nancy's paperwork up to date within three months and generally advanced the Social Development Department. The one thing I knew about Linda was that she got bored doing mundane activities. In the outside world, she was a rock concert promoter. She was always engaged in financial deals, even if a little larceny was required. Nancy allowed Linda to take over the inmate purchasing activities. At the time, a small group of inmates filled out requisition papers to purchase items from a small pharmacy and retail store. One day, Nancy escorted Linda on an escorted temporary pass to buy some special supplies for Social Development. Linda talked Nancy into taking her to a large department store so she could meet the people processing catalogue orders and offer her ideas on how the program could be expanded and improved if inmate purchases were included. No one in the institution was aware of Linda's plans to expand the inmate purchasing activity and obtain greater volumes.

Because of her gift for conversation and her skills in convincing people that she was working on their behalf, Linda saw an opportunity to expand the program and line her pockets with financial gain. It was the perfect sting arrangement. She had intimate knowledge of inmates' spending accounts and had a supervisor that was either too busy to handle the details of inmate accounts or preferred to trust Linda to work out the details. Linda did exactly that. She encouraged many inmates to purchase new items from the catalogue of a large national department store. Within one month, there were a few orders from the small local retail store. In three months, Linda had increased inmate purchasing from $500 to $2,000 per month. Linda worked really hard to satisfy the slow, unsuspecting inmates. She got them to make small purchases for goods they did not really need.

Linda became very aware that inmates had a second savings account where families and loved ones deposited money for the inmate's personal use. To get money from this account, the inmate had to sign a transfer document that was forwarded to the finance department in the prison. Linda saw opportunity for major fraud.

Linda had all the information she needed. She was aware that a certain inmate had $2,000 in her savings account and that some of this money could be transferred to purchase personal items. She was especially interested in inmates of low intelligence. In a very short time, Linda was forging inmates' signatures for money transfers. At Christmastime, Linda had increased inmate purchasing to $5,000 per month.

There was no stopping Linda now. She gained the trust of several hard-core drug addicts with appetites for larceny who helped her to obtain more expensive items and financial gain. Linda would forge an inmate's signature and order a watch worth $150; when it was received, the two assistants would find a willing person in the population to buy the watch for $50 cash. In time, with purchasers' credits and items returned, the department store was out $10,000 per month. To make things worse, Linda arranged some slow-minded inmates to open charge accounts at the department store with phony addresses.

One early morning, I received a telephone call from a mother of an intellectually challenged inmate. She complained that her daughter's account was down to $300 from a high of $2,000. Further, she explained that the daughter had no clothes or goods to show for the money being taken out of the savings account. I alerted the Assistant Warden of Finance about the potential problem. Several days later, he told me that $50,000 had been transferred out of inmates' accounts in the past year. He telephoned the head of the department store and learned that the department store's catalogue department was out many thousands of dollars.

Linda was fired from her job as clerk to the Head of Social Development. The police were called in, and fraud charges were laid against Linda. She was convicted and received another three years. Her fraud activities were so large that they made it into the Government of Canada Inspector General's annual report. It was a major wake-up call. In the future, inmates would not be making any decisions on inmate accounts or any other financial transactions.

Inmate Committee Chairpersons

Over the years, I encountered a number of inmates who were elected by their peers as Chairperson of the Inmate Committee. I found that an effective chairperson could have a positive influence on how the institution ran day by day. A negative chairperson with her own agenda could have the opposite result. The inmates who were attracted to this post were usually bright and enjoyed the benefits of one of the highest-paying inmate work positions in the institution. Some inmates enjoyed the highlights and frequent media requests for interviews on one topic or another. Chairpersons were usually in place for about one to two years. Sometimes a given inmate was elected as range representative and after one year could seek the chairperson position. I always stressed to inmates who sought the elected positions of range representative and chairperson that if they were found guilty of a major disciplinary offence, they would be off the committee. I was very firm on this matter and refused to meet with the committee if one or two members were found guilty of major disciplinary offences.

I found that if inmate leaders were committing serious institutional disciplinary offences, inmates in the population would not trust them or give them respect. Equally, if an inmate was found guilty of disciplinary offences, I would lose confidence in her ability to speak for the inmate population. It was a difficult balance to maintain. In my opinion, an effective chairperson was one who fought fairly for inmates' rights. She knew when negative inmates were lying and asking her to travel down a winding road where pitfalls were in abundance or there were no positive outcomes. I remember my predecessor telling me something that I will never forget. He said, "There is nothing more difficult and unequal than the equal treatment of unequal inmates."

I have fond memories of Billy Jo as Chairperson of the Inmate Committee in 1984. Billy Jo was a thirty-three-year-old black American lady from the Virgin Islands. She was an intelligent, attractive inmate who had striking black hair with long braids falling down her shoulders. She had beautiful facial features. Billy Jo could have been a model. Her smile and laugh were infectious.

Billy Jo was one of seven Americans in the prison. She was serving ten years for drug importation. She was caught at the airport with $200,000 worth of high-grade cocaine after exiting a plane from Europe. Billy Jo had the ability to communicate and make her points understood. She was elected vice-chairperson after four months in the prison. The chairperson then received a full parole, so after six months, Billy Jo became the Chairperson of the Inmate Committee. She had five members representing the living units, one member representing the Native Sisterhood, and one member who was a recreation representative. I met monthly with the Inmate Committee. Every month, the committee met with representatives of the Elizabeth Fry Society and with the Citizen Advisory Committee.

I invited Billy Jo to my office after she was elected. It was important that I find out more about this American inmate. She appeared at my office at exactly 3:00 p.m., the scheduled time for our meeting. I liked her right away. She spoke openly and let me know in no uncertain terms what was on her mind. She was motivated to do a good job and represented the population with no bias or preconceived opinions. She wanted straight talk and was willing to be reciprocal. I was totally off guard when Billy Jo made this request: "Warden, I want to do my job differently that the last chairperson. I would like to meet with you one-on-one every week for an informal meeting."

I thought about it and said, "Let's try it."

She commented, "No agenda—just straight talk."

I met with Billy Jo every week for one hour. I always arranged to have coffee available. She told me that she would look after inmate interests as long as I looked after staff concerns. After a number of informal meetings with Billy Jo, I knew I could count on her to give the straight goods to the population. Billy Jo went to bat for the hardened, difficult inmates as well as the inmates with low intelligence, and especially represented the foreign inmates who spoke little English. She always seemed to travel the middle road. She was well aware that I could not make decisions that would adversely affect the security of the institution.

During our eighteenth informal weekly meeting, Billy Jo had one special request. She was asked by an inmate named Roberta with a serious drug problem to ask me to allow her black common-law husband to have a family visit in the little house. The staff had denied her request three months before, because he had a history of drug convictions. Billy Jo told me that Roberta wanted the visit because she was pregnant with twin babies and wanted to tell her husband privately, in the quiet of the little house. Billy Jo stated that Roberta's husband had said that if she got pregnant they would give up drugs together.

Billy Jo was very concerned about Roberta's mental health. She emphasized that Roberta needed this visit. I asked Billy Jo how we could approve this request. Billy Joe knew that the staff concerns were realistic and that Roberta's drug addiction was a serious concern. She proposed something that might be able to win over staff support. She stated that if necessary, Roberta was willing to take a urine test for drug detection for five straight weeks. Furthermore her husband, who was at a halfway house where urine testing was scheduled weekly, was willing to share his results with prison staff. I told Billy Jo it might work. If Roberta and her husband had negative urine test results for five weeks, I would support the family visit.

Billy Jo thought that Roberta would be able to conceal her pregnancy until she met with her husband. I told Billy Jo I wanted to run this proposal pass the AW security and IPSO, as well as Roberta's classification officer. All three agreed to support the visit. After five weeks of negative urine test results for drug residue, I approved the family visit. The pregnancy helped bond the relationship between Roberta and her common-law husband. Within six and a half months Roberta, who had been released from prison, gave birth to healthy twin boys. Roberta and her husband received full paroles. Five years after giving birth to twins, both Roberta and her husband were working full time as drug counsellors in a large drug rehabilitation centre in Toronto.

After eight months into her term as Chairperson of the Inmate Committee, Billy Jo approached me in my office and said that she had a problem. She drew my attention to an inmate who was recently sentenced to thirty days in segregation for assaulting a staff member, being intoxicated, and destroying government property. The independent chairperson (ICP)[22] sentenced this inmate (Rosie) to thirty days in dissociation,[23] which was the full extent of the ICP's authority. The only thing the ICP could do to increase the sentence was to levy an additional fine for Rosie to pay for the damages and to suspend additional time in segregation if she maintained good behaviour.

Billy Jo told me that Rosie had found out that her parents, sister, and cousin were travelling to Ontario to visit her in two weeks. Billy Jo knew the policy that any inmate in dissociation did not receive visits until the sentence had been served. I asked what was so important about this case. Billy Joe visited inmates in segregation on a weekly basis and was told by Rosie that her parents were separated many years before and had recently got back together. Furthermore, Rosie was their only child, since Rosie's sister had been killed in an automobile accident about two years before. This visit would mean so much to Rosie.

After discussing this case with Rosie's classification officer and the chaplain, as well as the security staff, the decision was not opposed. In exceptional cases, the warden could override a decision of the ICP. I ran the details pass the ICP. She was an intelligent woman who was well aware that sometimes the warden had to act to balance the inmate's needs with the sentence given by the ICP. After a lot of soul-searching, I decided to suspend the inmate segregation sentence after two weeks of good behaviour. The day Rosie was released from segregation, her family arrived in Kingston. She had a good visit with her family for three straight days. These visits helped her relationship with her family. Rosie cleaned up her act and was released on full parole in six months.

---

22 The ICPs were mainly lawyers who entered the prison and chaired the disciplinary court.

23 When an inmate is found guilty and sentenced by an ICP in disciplinary court, the inmate is placed on punitive status (dissociation) and taken to segregation for a number of days.

Billy Jo cornered me in the gymnasium one afternoon and thanked me for the support I gave to Rosie. Billy Jo was the most effective chairperson I ever encountered. For fifteen months, the institution ran free of major problems. I gave a lot of credit to Billy Jo, who put out fires before they got larger. The population respected her and brought many items to her attention. In some cases, she told the population that their request was unreasonable and that the warden could not accept what they were asking.

I remember another chairperson with different consequences. After Billy Jo left her position, another inmate—one who identified with the hardened inmates—took control of the inmate committee. One Friday night, four months later, the majority of the inmate committee were stoned on drugs and placed in segregation. I accepted the chairperson's and vice-chairperson's letters of resignation.

The next chairperson was a difficult woman to understand and work with. The new chairperson was named May Lee, a forty-two-year-old half-Chinese, half-European woman who was serving a life sentence for killing her husband's second wife. May Lee was very intelligent, but always seemed to have ulterior motives behind her decision making.

May Lee was a stockbroker by profession and had her own investment agency in Saskatoon. She applied for the chairperson's job for reasons that she kept to herself. She was selfish and interested in money and power. She seemed to be moving the ship in a certain direction. She was very manipulative and took complete control of the Inmate Committee. May Lee could not simply do her time. She always seemed worried about her business and her husband.

About five years into May Lee's sentence, she received the bad news that her husband, who lived in Saskatoon, had suffered a stroke or a heart attack. May Lee knew she had to get back West to run her business and look after her husband. For the life of me, I could never determine what was more important, her stocks and financial business or her husband's health issues. May Lee applied for a parole with exception, but it was denied.

She became fanatical in her dealing with this matter. She wrote letters to various crime reporters of major Canadian newspapers, to politicians of all three parties in Ottawa, and to human rights lawyers. She tried every trick in the book to gain her release. May Lee was getting desperate. She was the Chairperson of the Inmate Committee, but her time seemed preoccupied with her release and little to do with inmate concerns.

May Lee could be very persuasive and managed to get what she required. She convinced a psychiatrist that she was mentally ill and needed help. Getting nowhere, May Lee tried another desperate tactic. She stopped eating and wrote letters stating that she would die in prison of starvation. She lost twelve pounds. On her small frame, a loss of twelve pounds was noticeable. May Lee wrote the Solicitor General and the Commissioner of the Correctional Service of Canada. The psychiatrist started writing letters to influence people. She argued that she needed to be near her ill husband, who was in a hospital in Saskatoon.

After many weeks of lobbying, May Lee was transferred to the Regional Treatment Centre in Saskatoon. This was an unusual move, since no female prisoners were at this facility. May Lee later filed a complaint with the Canadian Human Rights Commission, citing discrimination against female federal inmates. She used this tactic to gain her transfer. Her lawyer argued that a woman could not transfer across Canada to be near an ill relative, since the PFW was the only female federal prison in Canada. Male inmates, on the other hand, could transfer to a male prison in another province to be near relatives.

I was surprised that CSC set up a special room at the Regional Treatment Centre for May Lee to reside in until she was eligible for day parole. May Lee received escorted temporary absences to see her husband and, when the time arrived, she was granted day parole and then full parole. May Lee knew how to push senior correctional authorities and cabinet ministers in the government in Ottawa.

I suspected CSC did not want an international incident on their hands if May Lee were to die. Her Canadian Human Rights complaint was gaining momentum and was discussed by higher authorities. May Lee used the system to get what she wanted, but her performance as Chairperson of the Inmate Committee was less than expected and not effective in moving the needs of the population. I will give her credit in that her complaint had merit and revealed that there were differences between male and female inmates in terms of program opportunities and physical housing arrangements. Inmates like May Lee would never be satisfied with the Criminal Justice System. Yes, we had problems, but some inmates entered the prison system and came with deep-rooted psychological and mental health issues that would never be appropriately resolved or ameliorated while they were young. A prison environment was the final depository of those with scarred human frailties who resent their past reality.

Mary Ann's Release on Full Day Parole

Mary Ann's last few weeks on conditional day parole at the prison were uneventful. She would wake early in the morning, shower, have breakfast, and take the bus to the college. Mary Ann enjoyed her courses. During her first semester, Mouse reported that she was taking technical math, technical writing, blueprint reading, land use planning, and construction drafting. With the exception of construction drafting, Mary Ann found the courses really difficult. Given that she had never attended high school, Mary Ann felt that she had more work to catch up on. She had lots of reading and homework every night. Mary Ann did not have much time for socialization. She had supper with Jamie each night, but once they returned to the wing, she went to her room to study and complete assignments. Mary Ann stated she would stay up until eleven p.m. most nights, and some nights she would go to bed at one a.m. Mary Ann remarked that looking back, she could sense that Jamie was becoming less and less involved with her life.

Surprisingly, the last two days in the institution went by easily. Mary Ann purchased a Saint Lawrence College ring and a small gold chain and gave them to Jamie the night before she left the prison. Jamie gave her a good-quality drafting pencil and ruler set. Jamie helped Mouse pack the night before she left the institution. Mary Ann had come to the prison with a small bag of clothes, a few small personal items, and two photos of her children. She was leaving the Prison for Women with five boxes, including one large box of books, music, and pictures.

The next morning, Jamie went for breakfast with Mouse. After they walked back to the wing area, Jamie helped Mouse put her five boxes on a small cart. Inside Mary Ann's cell, Jamie gave her a really good hug and kissed her on the lips. Jamie quickly said, "I love you." Mouse felt a little empty. She hugged Jamie and told her that she was a true friend. She thanked Jamie for all her help and support. She stated that she would write and update Jamie on what was happening with her life. Jamie would be leaving the prison in eight months if the National Parole Board granted her full parole.

Jamie helped Mouse deliver her property to the front foyer of the prison. After expressing their goodbyes again, Jamie left with a small tear in her eye. She went up upstairs to the chapel to watch Mouse walk away from the prison.

As the final gate opened, the older guard in the control post, who had been there when Mary Ann first entered the prison, yelled through the little hole in the Plexiglas window, "Good luck, Mary Ann. You have done well here. Kick butt and finish your studies!"

The door closed. The institutional driver helped Mary Ann load her personal belongings into the van. Mary Ann mentioned that she held her composure until she sat down in the back seat of the van. As the van pulled away, she looked up and saw Jamie place a sign in the chapel window on the third floor. It said, "I love you." A few tears fell to her lap as the van sped away.

Mary Ann arrived at the Elizabeth Fry Society halfway house at 9:15 a.m. The halfway house was located on a quiet street in a working-class area of Kingston. The residence was relatively new and was surrounded by older houses on both sides of the street. The halfway house had eight bedrooms. The house supervisor welcomed Mouse into her new home. There were five other women in the house. Mary Ann was assigned a large bedroom on the second floor. There was a second bed and desk in the bedroom, but they were not occupied. The house supervisor stated that the second bed would be filled in five weeks. She gave Mary Ann a little speech on the rules of the halfway house. She advised Mary Ann that her parole officer was out of town and would see her late Monday afternoon. After fifteen minutes, Mary Ann's belongings were brought upstairs. An older inmate that Mary Ann knew gave her a brief tour of the facility and showed her how to operate the laundry's washer and dryer. Four other women who lived in the house were attending school or at work.

Mary Ann felt a little uncomfortable. She was apprehensive of a younger inmate that lived in the house. This inmate was a close friend of the two French inmates that had cornered Mary Ann in the washroom after she was first transferred to the wing area of the prison. This young inmate had a history of assault. She resided on the second floor as well, but her bedroom was at the end of the hallway. She shared her bedroom with a lifer who had been released from the prison a year ago.

Mary Ann had lunch with the older woman who had given her the tour and the house supervisor. Each inmate prepared her own breakfast and lunch. Mary Ann, like other residents, participated in preparing the evening meal. She was fortunate in that she had Saturday and Sunday to get acclimatized to her new lodgings and assess her housemates.

Given the nature of her offence, Mary Ann was a little apprehensive being in the house. In the afternoon, she unpacked her bags. She was happy that she had her own desk with a small lamp. She sat down after finishing putting her things away and wrote a small note to Jamie. At supper, there were six people enjoying the shared meal. Each resident helped to prepare the meal. The inmate that Mary Ann was concerned about was away on a pass to her grandmother's house located near Toronto. She was expected back late Sunday night.

Mary Ann was not accustomed to a firm mattress. She opened her window and slept wonderfully. On Sunday morning, one resident left early to attend church. This was an unusual situation. Few inmates seemed to attend weekly service in the prison. Mary Ann went for a long walk. She walked for two hours around the neighbourhood. She asked directions to where the closest library was located. She found that the central library was the easiest to get to and had regular bus service to the front door. In the late afternoon, Mary Ann went to her room and read her textbooks and completed assignments. There was no class on Friday, because the teaching staff were attending staff development meetings.

Mary Ann had not prepared a meal in over six years. She found it exciting and exhilarating. She watched the other residents and picked up clues on how to prepare certain foods. She commented that in her opinion it was a good idea for the residents to prepare the evening meals. Her job was to peel potatoes and cut up some carrots. She was also responsible for making some orange juice.

Sunday night, Mary Ann went to bed early. Attending classes the next morning would be a new experience. She had to walk to the corner in order to take the bus to the college. The inmate that she was concerned about had arrived at the residence after ten p.m. when Mary Ann was asleep.

The next morning, Mary Ann prepared a few sandwiches and headed for the bus stop early. The bus was on time. Mary Ann arrived at the college at 8:50 a.m. Her first class was at 9:00 a.m. She had three classes in the morning and one hour for lunch before her next class. She walked to the cafeteria with her bag over her shoulder. Mary Ann waited in line to get a drink. As she was waiting in line, a good-looking man in his early thirties who was standing near her asked her what she was studying. She turned around, and their eyes locked. Mary Ann felt uncomfortable. She spoke slowly, "I am studying Architecture Technology. What are you studying?"

He responded, "I'm studying Business."

Mary Ann was ahead of this man in the line and paid for her drink. She walked up to the counter but did not know how to operate the new machine. A voice followed her. "Lift up the handle and the pop will come out. Put your paper cup under the nozzle." It worked. Mary Ann got her drink and sat down at a table located across the large cafeteria. She drank her pop then headed for her class. She finished her last class at 3:15 p.m. She had time to go to the bookstore and get a small book on urban planning. She made the four p.m. bus heading downtown. Mary Ann met her parole supervisor, Shannon, who was employed by the Elizabeth Fry Society. Shannon reported indirectly to a federal parole supervisor who was located in Kingston. Shannon was about thirty-nine years old and had worked with female offenders for twelve years.

Mary Ann and Shannon got off to a good start. Mary Ann talked about her school situation and her apprehensions. She mentioned that she was a little concerned about Carole, who lived down the hall. Shannon responded, "Don't worry about Carole. She puts up a tough impression. She wants to go home to Vancouver at the end of next month. She will not get herself into anybody's business. She wants to go home on full parole."

Shannon's words resonated with Mary Ann. She was reassured that Carole had her own agenda and would not likely even acknowledge her. Later that night at supper, Carole surprised Mary Ann by asking her how she enjoyed Saint Lawrence College. Mary Ann quickly answered, "I enjoy my classes, but since I have been out of school for many years, I am finding my studies difficult. I have signed up for a tutor that meets me several times during the week." Mary Ann felt that Carole was interested in talking a little bit, but that she had her own agenda.

The next day, Mary Ann had several mid-term exams. She was getting only "C" grades and needed a lot of help. Vivian, who was twenty-four years old, was an excellent tutor and a math whiz who was completing her second degree in civil engineering. She was an "A" student and really helped Mary Ann understand her homework assignments. Mary Ann was determined to be successful and obtain her degree regardless of how much work it required.

Bomb Threat

Some days the prison was quiet and as still as the water of a pristine virgin lake high up in a mountain range. Equally, the prison could erupt like a volcano within an instant. Working in a prison, you were like an excited roller-coaster rider: one moment you were in ecstasy and the next moment you could fall asleep in a soft turn.

In early May 1986, the prison experienced an exciting day. The Solicitor General (Sol Gen) of Canada and seven of his staff, several high-profile politicians, were arriving from Ottawa to visit the Kingston Penitentiary and the Prison for Women. We were first to have the Sol Gen visit our institution. His travel itinerary was probably known to only a small group of his staff, his secretary, senior staff at Regional Headquarters, and maybe someone in the prime minister's office. Given the increasing profile of the Prison for Women and interest from opposition political leaders, it was good politics to visit the institution to see the inmates and the administrative officials. You never knew when an incident would erupt in the House of Commons and reach the Solicitor General's desk.

The senior staff and I were waiting for the Sol Gen and his entourage to arrive. We were told that they would be in the institution before 9:30 a.m. At 9:45 a.m., I was contacted by the correctional officer in the front control centre and advised that the Sol Gen and his staff had arrived in the parking lot and would be in the institution shortly. I introduced myself to the group and welcomed them to the Prison for Women. After the official greeting, I asked the Sol Gen and his staff to join my senior staff and myself for coffee in the chapel. The introduction of my senior staff went fine. I was explaining some of the current issues facing the staff in the management of some difficult inmates. After briefing the Sol Gen for twenty minutes, the senior staff and I were prepared to answer any questions the Sol Gen might have. He had begun to ask relevant questions of interest to himself when a correctional supervisor entered the room. She said it was urgent and that she needed to speak to me. I exited the room for a minute to hear what she had to say.

She said, "Warden, we just received a bomb threat over the telephone." She went on to say that an unidentified female caller had informed them that a bomb would go off in the prison before 10:15 a.m.—in nine minutes. I directed the correctional supervisor to contact the Kingston City Police and alert the RCMP as well. One of the eight staff members with the Sol Gen was an RCMP plainclothes police officer. I directed that we should vacate the prison immediately. I suggested that the inmates be directed to exit into the institution's main yard. I further directed that a complete count be conducted. Inmates in segregation were to be escorted to the small outside exercise yard at the bottom of the range.

I entered the room and interrupted the Sol Gen as he was speaking. I said that we had just received a telephone bomb threat and we were taking the matter seriously. I directed that everyone in the chapel travel down the back stairs to the ground area behind the visiting and correspondence area. I left the group. The AW Security escorted the Sol Gen and his guests down the stairs. I went to my office to manage the crisis. The police arrived within four minutes. I informed the staff sergeant of the Kingston City Police that all staff, inmates, and guests had exited the building and a head count was being conducted. I told the police officer that the bomb was to go off in five minutes. The police sergeant called in members of the bomb squad. I had told him that we had the Sol Gen and his staff in the institution. The police listened to the tape and were convinced of its authenticity.

Several members of the bomb squad arrived within fifteen minutes and searched the institution. The nine minutes had passed, and no bomb had gone off. After searching the building, the police felt it was safe for the inmates, staff, and guests to reenter the institution. The Sol Gen thanked me for conducting a quick exodus of inmates and personnel. The Sol Gen also thanked me for the brief meeting and said that he and his staff were invited for lunch at Kingston Penitentiary and that he wished he could stay longer. The bomb threat helped to motivate our guests to take their leave of us.

The bomb threat tape was reviewed by experts, but no charges were laid. Some staff were convinced that the verbal bomb threat came from an inmate who had recently been released from the prison. The one good result from the bomb threat was that it served as an excellent opportunity to evaluate our crisis management model. We cleared the entire prison in five minutes. In fact, some staff and inmates thought it was all arranged to impress the Sol Gen!

In all my years at the Prison for Women, this was the only bomb threat that I ever encountered. One week later, I had several senior police officers from the Kingston City Police and the bomb squad members meet with us to discuss the incident. The AW Security and I ran through the entire scenario to see if there was anything that we could have done differently. We changed our electronic equipment to better record and possibly identify the phone number and location of the incoming calls. The exercise helped some inmates to realize that CSC treats bomb threats seriously, and that human life must be protected.

One week later, I received a card from the Sol Gen. He felt bad and stated that during his next visit to Kingston he would complete arrangements to visit the PFW. Within six months, the cabinet had changed. The Sol Gen was reassigned to another portfolio during a cabinet shuffle.

8

Mary Ann's College Experiences

Mary Ann enjoyed her daily bus trips to and from the college. She got her marks back from her mid-term exams. She received a "C" average. She did not do well in her math exam. In order to improve her math mark, Mary Ann met Vivian, her tutor, on Tuesdays, Wednesdays, and Thursdays during lunch.

One Friday, Mary Ann went to the cafeteria in order to get a drink. As she was waiting in line, she heard someone call to her. "How are your classes going?" She turned her head and noticed that it was the same man who had helped her previously to work the drink machine.

Mary Ann replied, "They are going okay, but I could do better." Mary Ann was in a good mood this day. The man asked her to join him for lunch. She accepted. They sat at the last table near the window. The young man spoke first. "By the way, my name is Brian. What's your name?"

She answered, "Mary Ann." The two talked for about twenty-five minutes, at which time Brian said he had to go and set up his class project. Mary Ann reported that she enjoyed Brian's company and was a bit curious about his background. She observed that he had a tattoo of a skeleton on his forearm and that he had no ring on his left finger. She concluded that he might be single.

Mary Ann did not see Brian again for two weeks. She again met him during the lunch break in the cafeteria. That day, she invited Brian to join her. She was in a very good mood. She had received a "B" on her math exam. Brian told her that he was from Calgary, Alberta, and was in the second year of his business program. He said he had worked in the oil patch, but wanted to do something more in tune with his interests. So he moved to Toronto and worked for an investment financial company. Brian said that he was single. He was married, he said, very early, but his young wife died during childbirth, and so did the baby.

Mary Ann did not reveal too much of herself. She told Brian that she was living with a friend of her aunt's. Brian enjoyed her company and asked her if she would join him for breakfast on Saturday morning. Mary Ann hesitated then said, "I can't this week, but I will meet you next Saturday morning." Mary Ann was now more comfortable with Brian and looked forward in meeting him for breakfast.

Mary Ann agreed to meet Brian at nine a.m. at a small café located in the shopping centre. She enjoyed herself and even laughed when he told a funny joke. They talked for an hour and drank two cups of coffee. Brian said that he had no girlfriend and enjoyed her company. He asked her to go the movies the following Friday night. Mary Ann did not give a firm answer. She said that if she got her work done, she would enjoy going to a movie. She especially enjoyed Harrison Ford's movies.

It was early December, and Mary Ann had her final semester exams coming up. She saw Brian one lunch hour and said she would enjoy going to a movie. She told him that she would study at the school library until 6:30 p.m., at which time he could meet her in front of the college. He agreed. Brian had no car, so they took a taxi to the movies. They enjoyed the movie and afterwards went for a hamburger in a café located nearby.

Mary Ann enjoyed herself and was becoming attracted to Brian. She said she lived far out in the east end of the city and preferred to take a bus. Brian at first did not want her to take a bus, but she convinced him that it would be better if she went home by bus. Brian told Mary Ann his last name was Black. He asked to see her again. He asked for her telephone number, but she declined, saying her aunt's friend did not want her to give the telephone number to anybody.

Mary Ann saw Brian at school three times at lunch during the next two weeks. She completed her exams and felt confident that she had done very well. Brian told her that he was going home to Alberta for Christmas, but he hoped to see her around New Year's. He left a friend's telephone number so she could call him near the end of the month. Brian gave her a Christmas card with a poem inside and a gift card to buy her two favourite music selections. He kissed her on the cheek and left the building. Mary Ann mentioned that she felt that there was something mysterious about Brian. She really enjoyed his company, but held back.

Jennifer's Story

During my years at the Prison for Women, there was one unique group of inmates that attracted my attention. In 1976 (July 26), the Government of Canada abolished the death penalty. Soon after, the prison started to receive women serving life sentences with no possibility of parole consideration until twenty-five years had been served.

I remember 1977, the year Jennifer arrived at the prison. Jennifer was the first woman convicted of first-degree murder (Section 218:[1] of the Criminal Code of Canada); she had killed a police officer in a large city in Western Canada. On March 12, 1976, Jennifer's husband and another man robbed a credit union bank and were trying to flee the city after the robbery. A police officer stopped their vehicle, which was driven by Jennifer, near the edge of the city, and soon a gun battle erupted. One of the male robbers who exited the vehicle shot the police officer, who died.

Jennifer and another woman as well as the two male accomplices were pursued by the police. The group took possession of three hostages in a private residence. The police cordoned the area. A long standoff occurred. The next night, the hostages were released. After a long wait, the police stormed the house. Jennifer's husband had overdosed on drugs and was found dead in the house. Jennifer and the one remaining male were taken into custody and charged with first-degree murder. The other woman was not charged by the police and was subsequently released. The police offered her amnesty or immunity from criminal charges during the negotiations with the hostage-takers. Jennifer's lawyer argued that she did not shoot the gun that killed the police officer and should not have been charged with first-degree murder.

But the law had changed after the abolishment of the death penalty. Jennifer was found guilty of a new section in the criminal code that basically said that a person who was present during a murder act was as guilty as the one who pulled the trigger. Jennifer and her co-accused were each convicted of first-degree murder with no chance of parole for twenty-five years (Section 7:45 of the Criminal Code of Canada).

Jennifer was an attractive twenty-two-year-old when she first entered the Prison for Women. She was cocky and full of confidence that she had been wrongly convicted and soon would be released. I reviewed Jennifer's file and observed that Jennifer and her husband used drugs and that their criminal activities most likely helped to support their lifestyle and illegal drug consumption.

Jennifer walked around the institution like a celebrity. She was the first woman to be convicted of first-degree murder and fed off her notoriety. She milked this reality in the prison and received a lot of press coverage. In the eyes of many misguided inmates, Jennifer was initially viewed as a hero and poster child for the inmate with the longest sentence.

I was not close to Jennifer. As warden, I was close to some inmates, but never close to them all. Some inmates did not trust police officers, correctional officers, assistant wardens, or the warden. Looking back, I found that each staff member had some inmates that they related well to and some others that they could not communicate with. I found Jennifer to be manipulative and cunning. She looked good, talked the talk, and gave a favourable first impression.

My predecessor had had a good relationship with Jennifer and tried to show her compassion and understanding. I was totally convinced that Jennifer was not forthcoming and completely honest. I viewed Jennifer as an inmate who had been found guilty of first-degree murder by the court. I really didn't judge her, whether or not she had pulled the trigger. I thought there was a crack in her armour. In my opinion, Jennifer had a serious, long-term drug problem and it was progressive. Her case management file revealed that she had been using drugs many months prior to her arrest. Given Jennifer's ability to talk and communicate, her story attracted converts to her cause. But I remained steadfast in my belief that Jennifer had a hidden personal fault. She had a problem with drugs.

Over the years, Jennifer became more cynical and negative. She felt betrayed by the justice system. She formed a relationship with another young, attractive girl named Gail. They both resided in the wing. Jennifer and Gail were always seen together. Gail was good for Jennifer and helped her during a difficult time in her life. After three years, Gail was released on parole. It was a sad day for Jennifer. Her anchor and best friend was leaving.

After Gail's departure, Jennifer's attitude seemed to take a turn for the worse. I don't know if she was depressed, but she seemed to give up her fight for justice. She started to associate more and more with known hard-core drug addicts.

The staff had received information periodically from inmate sources that suggested Jennifer was using drugs. Finding the drugs and obtaining evidence was not easy to do. Each time Jennifer was charged with being under the influence of an intoxicant, she appeared in disciplinary court. She was always defended by a Queen's University law professor who was an excellent defence lawyer. I think both the defence lawyer and Jennifer knew it was important that she not be found guilty of a drug offence in the prison. I suspect her lawyer would find it to be an undesirable liability for his client, who was appealing her conviction, to have charges and sentences in disciplinary court for drug-related offences. Jennifer's lawyer was tireless in his defence of her charges.

I clearly remember an event in 1985 that had a serious repercussion. One morning, the AW Security came to my office and talked about some events that had occurred during the previous night. The AW Security related that a new correctional officer had charged Jennifer with being under the influence of intoxicants and possession of a homemade brew that was found in her room. First thing in the morning, Jennifer called her lawyer and put in a request to have a legal representative at the disciplinary hearing. Given the backlog of cases, Jennifer was scheduled for disciplinary court in two weeks.

The next morning, the AW Security came to my office and was visibly upset. She explained, "Officer Jones was pressured last night by Jennifer and her friends to drop the charges against Jennifer." I indicated firmly that if this had actually occurred, Officer Jones would be finished here at the prison. I arranged for Mrs.

Jones to come to my office. She arrived within eight minutes. "Good morning, Mrs. Jones. How is your new job working out?" Mrs. Jones hesitated and started to cry. I said, "Please sit down. Is it true that you approached the correctional supervisor and wished to withdraw the charges against inmate Jennifer Smith? What happened last night while you were working in the wing?"

Mrs. Jones looked outside the window and spoke in a low tone. "Inmate Jennifer's friends swarmed me in the common room located in the wing area. She was fifteen feet away, but did not talk to me. It was clearly orchestrated by her. The five inmates who were identified said that if inmate Jennifer was found guilty of these charges, the appeal of her conviction might be put in jeopardy." The group of five inmates made it clear that they would make Mrs. Jones's work experience difficult. According to Mrs. Jones, they were not clear on this point.

I gave Mrs. Jones very serious look. I responded, "Listen, Mrs. Jones: If you capitulate and withdraw the charges, your effectiveness and authority as a correctional officer will be compromised, and your ability to work here will be finished. Do you understand what I am saying?"

She answered quickly, "Yes."

I looked directly at Mrs. Jones and said, "If you withdraw the charges against Jennifer, I want your letter of transfer or resignation before you leave work today."

Before leaving work, Mrs. Jones came to see me. "Mr. Caron, I decided to not withdraw the charges against inmate Jennifer."

Two weeks later, the two charges were heard in disciplinary court. The ICP, who was an experienced lawyer, listened attentively to the testimony of Mrs. Jones and the defence arguments submitted clearly by inmate Jennifer's lawyer. The ICP cleared the court with the exception of the senior correctional officer who managed the disciplinary court.

After fifteen minutes, the court hearing was reconvened. The ICP found inmate Jennifer not guilty because Correctional Officer Jones did not provide sufficient details about Jennifer's state of intoxication. Furthermore, Jennifer's lawyer presented evidence that she had received a new medication the day before the incident and it made her dizzy. A nurse was called to the hearing and stated that the medication sometimes caused dizziness. The charge of the brew was disallowed, as someone in the security office had mistakenly discarded the brew, which was in a garbage bag. Inmate Jennifer thanked her lawyer and retreated back to the wing. She later gave high fives to her friends and celebrated her positive outcome in court.

When I first started at the Prison for Women, disciplinary court was chaired by the warden. In the late seventies, the Correctional Service of Canada contracted out independent chairperson positions for disciplinary hearings to lawyers in the community. As the years progressed, the emphasis on due process was heightened. When the Charter of Rights was passed in Parliament (1982), legal defence lawyers pushed the justice folder by challenging a number of rulings in Federal Court on how the Correctional Service of Canada was conducting its business relating to inmate disciplinary hearings, charges, testimony, and evidence, and basically increased the due process requirements. If charges were not dealt with in a timely manner, they would be thrown out. An ICP was assigned a clerk and a duty counsel. Due process was now entrenched in the disciplinary process inside Canadian prisons. In recent years, there has been a significant reduction in Charter of Rights issues relating to the disciplinary hearing process.

Within one year, Correctional Officer Jones transferred to a male prison. Inmate Jennifer's skillful lawyer and a gifted constitutional lawyer finally obtained a positive decision on December 8, 1988, from the Supreme Court of Canada.[24] They argued that she had been charged before the Criminal Code of Canada was amended and that she should have been charged under the old Act. The court ruled that Jennifer was now eligible for parole upon the date of the release of the judgment. She would no longer have to wait for twenty-five years before she was eligible for parole. Inmate Jennifer was granted day parole in June 1989 (after serving about thirteen years) and full parole by the National Parole Board in January 1990. On September 29, 1990, or approximately

---

24 Supreme Court of Canada 1989, Judgment on Appeal for Ontario, Dec. 8, 1988.

ten months after she had been released on full parole, inmate Jennifer was killed in an automobile accident. She was in the same automobile with another woman who was an ex-inmate from the Prison for Women and who had a history of drug convictions.

Mary Ann's 1986 Christmas

Mary Ann had a quiet Christmas in 1986. She and another woman were the only residents in the house. Mary Ann and Mabel cooked a small turkey and prepared a nice meal. Mary Ann missed having people around to share the holiday season. Mary Ann had received a Christmas card from Jamie on December 23. Jamie had told her that she was applying for parole and hoped to be going out West before next July. Mary Ann told me that she had mailed a Christmas card to Jamie a few days before and hoped that she had received it. It included a picture of herself in front of Saint Lawrence College.

Mouse became depressed between Christmas and New Year's. There were few residents in the halfway house. She missed human contact. On December 30, she received a letter with her marks from the college. She was excited because she had passed all her courses and had received a C+ average for her first semester. Mary Ann related that she had received seventy percent on her math exam and was ecstatic. The same night, she telephoned the number that Brian had given her. A male answered, stating that Brian was at work but would be home at approximately ten p.m. She called back from a telephone booth that was located close to the residence. She reached Brian, and the two agreed to meet for dinner on January 1 at seven p.m. at a local restaurant.

Mary Ann walked to the restaurant and arrived a few minutes before seven. A few minutes later, Brian arrived. They were seated at their reserved table. Mary Ann and Brian drank a full bottle of red wine. They had a great meal. They both felt the alcohol's influence. They were talkative. Brian confided to Mary Ann that he had been an inmate at Frontenac Institution when he first met her, but was now on full parole.

Mary Ann had sensed there was something different about Brian. His tattoo gave him away. Brian explained that he had served one and one-half years of a three-year sentence for driving a friend's automobile while intoxicated and hitting a young couple walking on the street. The young couple were not hurt badly. He admitted that this was his second accident while intoxicated. Brian was excited. He had found a basement apartment and would be moving in about fourteen days. He also mentioned that he had obtained a part-time job at a building supply centre that was open until 10:00 p.m. every night.

Mary Ann thought about telling Brian that she was an inmate from the Prison for Women, but decided it was not the right time to share this information. She and Brian left the restaurant at about eleven p.m. Mary Ann made an excuse that she had to help her aunt's friend with some paperwork. They agreed to meet at the college for lunch on Friday, and took a cab to Brian's friend's place. Brian kissed Mary Ann and thanked her for a nice night and then exited the cab. Mary Ann told the taxi driver to drive to a house close to her residence.

Mary Ann saw Brian off and on at lunch hour during the next semester. He was busy with his courses and part-time employment. Several times he invited her for dinner and to see a movie. He had his own apartment, but never invited her over for dinner or to socialize. Mary Ann noted that letters received from Jamie were becoming fewer and fewer. She sent a note each month to give Jamie a briefing on her situation.

In mid-April, a new resident from the Prison for Women was admitted to the halfway house. Her named was Agnes. She was a shy woman about fifty ears old. She was serving two years and six months for fraud. One evening she said hello to Mary Ann and another resident. During the conversation, Agnes related that the previous weekend several inmates, including Jamie, her black girlfriend, and two French inmates got totally drunk and were placed in segregation. Agnes further related that Jamie had assaulted two correctional officers who were escorting her to segregation.

Mary Ann did not let on to Agnes that she had gone with Jamie last summer. She concluded that Jamie now had another girlfriend, and that was the reason why she wrote so few letters.

Mary Ann completed all her exams by the middle of April. During the last week of April, she received a letter from the college with her grades. She was very happy; she had received a

B average. She even got a B on her final math exam! The first year was finished. Mary Ann decided to take some courses during the summer months and reduce her study load for the second and final year of her program. Mary Ann was so excited that she telephoned Brian and asked him if he would like to celebrate her good grades. They agreed to meet at a restaurant at 7:15 p.m. after he had finished his work shift.

Mary Ann and Brian went to the first café they had attended together. Brian indicated that he had passed his exams as well. Brian told Mary Ann that he had received a full-time, high-paying job in the oil patch and had decided to return to Alberta in two days. He said that he would write her and see her in the fall.

Mary Ann felt that there was something else that was pulling Brian back to Alberta, and it wasn't money or a full-time job. She concluded that she would not get more involved with Brian until she got some answers. She signed up for two courses related to her program that were offered during the summer. The courses would run from late May to the first week in August.

Microfilm Program

During the eighties, a new program opportunity opened up for some female offenders who were in the last part of their sentence or close to day parole. The microfilm project that was created at Bath Minimum Security Institution (male prison) required additional workers for the expanding program. The work was somewhat technical in nature. Workers took important museum and archive paper documents and transposed their images into microfilm strips. The inmates were asked to apply for this new work and training opportunity. Eight mature, intelligent inmates were selected to work on the project. They would be compensated more highly than they would earn at other prison jobs.

The inmates were bused each morning from the prison at 8:00 a.m. and transported approximately twenty-five miles to the Bath Institution. The inmates were escorted by correctional officers each day and returned at 3:30 p.m. This work opportunity was perfect for inmates who wanted to get out of the prison and experience as nearly as possible a normal work routine. Some inmates told me the best part of their prison experience was the daily bus trip down the winding highway alongside Lake Ontario. It is a very scenic view and filled with many beautiful images of water, boats, and waterfowl. As for some of the others, they enjoyed working alongside male inmates on their technical tasks.

We never experienced any major problems with the inmates participating in the program. Over the months, one female inmate and one male inmate were removed from the program because they appeared to be involved with one another and were more interested in each other than in the work. I always worried about drugs being smuggled into the prison. There were more male inmates receiving daily passes into the community than the Prison for Women. They had easier access to illegal drugs than did the female inmates. I must admit we had our suspicions, but the female workers in this project rarely missed work, and there was no physical evidence that they were using drugs.

I clearly remember one inmate that worked on the project. Marika was a beautiful, wealthy, thirty-five-year-old woman from Lebanon who was serving seven years for drug importation. The day Marika was being released from the prison to be deported back to the Middle East, she asked to see me. Marika had worked on the microfilm project for almost two years. Her institutional record was without incident. Marika told me that I had treated her fairly and that she appreciated the opportunity to work on the microfilm project. It was for this reason she wanted to pass on some information. Marika told me that several drug addicts in the wing had asked her to take some drugs into the prison from Bath Institution. She refused on several occasions.

One day she was told that if she did not do as they wanted, she would have her pretty face cut open like a sardine can. Given that she feared for her safety, Marika agreed to smuggle drugs into the prison only once. She admitted that the previous week she had smuggled in a small bag of cocaine. Because she was trusted by the guards, she was not searched as closely as other inmates. She concealed the drugs in her panties. She was relieved when she entered the prison without being apprehended. We searched the wing area that afternoon and found several small bags of drugs concealed in several areas but not located inside inmate's cells.

Given this information, the staff started searching closely all inmates from the Bath project. Inmates were asked to take off their clothes, which were searched for drugs.

The microfilm project was an excellent work experience for some inmates and helped prepare them for their eventual release to the community. However, there is always someone who will take advantage of every situation.

More about Mouse

Mary Ann enjoyed her summer months. There were six residents in the house. Another resident joined her every morning on the bus to the college, where they took summer courses.

The summer went quickly. Soon it was early September. Mary Ann was disappointed that she had received only one letter from Brian, and it had no forwarding address. He indicated that he was working on a drilling rig located in a very isolated part of Alberta. Brian did say he was making lots of money and would be getting a larger apartment; one that was bigger than the matchbox basement apartment that he had rented last semester.

Mary Ann started the second year of her program with great confidence and aspirations. She looked forward to the day when she could work for a large architecture or engineering firm. One afternoon, I could not believe my eyes. Mary Ann was walking up to the front door at the prison! I immediately thought the worst. I really surmised that Mary Ann was pulling the plug and wanted to come back into the prison. Maybe she had received a letter from Jamie asking her to return.

I was completely wrong. I forgot that inmates on day parole at the Elizabeth Fry Society had to return to the prison for health care issues. The Chief of Health Care was very protective of her health care budget. Mrs. Thomas did not want inmates in the community to make unnecessary visits to outside medical clinics that had additional health care staff like a physiotherapist, occupational therapist, foot specialist, etc. Mrs. Thomas wanted to control the costs associated with health care. If an inmate on day parole required additional medical attention, a referral would be made by the institutional physician.

I saw Mary Ann briefly when she entered the front door. She was seeing the institutional physician to discuss a female medical problem. I commented that Mary Ann looked good and definitely passed as a college sophomore. Mary Ann mentioned that she was back at school and that things were going fine. Jamie did not know that Mouse had come into the Health Care Centre.

9

Health Care at the PFW

Prior to 1977, the Prison for Women had one part-time physician who came from Kingston Penitentiary three half-days per week. Inmates who required dental work had to be escorted to Kingston Penitentiary, where the service was provided. How things changed over the years after Mrs. Thomas took over as Chief of Health Care in 1977!

Prison for Women entrance, 1965; the Health Care Centre takes up the second floor.

In 1978, the P4W had its own institutional physician, on contract, three half-days per week. The physician was on call at other times as well and could be reached for emergencies and changes to medication orders. A psychiatrist attended the institution three half-days per week. Further, the inmates could see a dentist three half-days each week in the Health Care Centre at the P4W.

In 1986, a female physician, on contract, took over as the institutional physician. By the end of 1986, Mrs. Thomas had a pharmacist, a physiotherapist, and an optometrist on board, part time. The inmates were well served with full-time registered nurses working around the clock. In many instances, inmates received better health-care services than they received in their home communities.

Mary Ann and Brian

Mary Ann had completed three weeks at Saint Lawrence College and had not yet seen Brian. During the fourth week, she found him sitting alone in the cafeteria. He was completely surprised to see her. He remarked that he had lost her address and had no telephone number. Furthermore, he indicated that he was working part time most evenings from five until ten p.m. Brian kissed her on the cheek and seemed genuinely interested in seeing her. He gave her his new telephone number and his new address. They agreed to go out on Saturday evening. Once again, Mary Ann felt something was not right and that Brian was holding back. Mary Ann had known Brian for over one year, and he had not pursued sex. She cared for Brian and wanted to become intimate with him.

Brian invited Mary Ann to visit him at his apartment the first week in October. Brian said that he would cook for her the best steak dinner he could create. Mary Ann took a taxi to Brian's house that Saturday night. She wore a revealing shirt and put on her best dress pants and accessories. Brian noticed his prize when she entered his apartment. It was a nice apartment that had a beautiful view of the lake. They had a glass of red wine and sat outside on the balcony. Brian had a beautiful classical Chopin piano piece playing when she entered the living room. She asked him, "Who is playing this beautiful sonata?" "Oh, it is a Canadian artist named Glenn Gould." Mary Ann stated that he was her favourite. After two bottles of red wine and a good meal, Mary Ann was carried into the bedroom, where they made passionate love for two hours. They sat in the bed and talked about their life. Mary Ann thought about it but never revealed her background.

The relationship with Brian improved. During the next six weeks, Mary Ann had dinner each Saturday night at his apartment. On Sunday they would go for long walks along the lake. Soon it was the second week of December, and Mary Ann was writing her exams for the semester. Brian saw Mary Ann in the cafeteria during the lunch hour on Friday. He surprised her again. He said, "Mary Ann, I have been offered an opportunity to work on the oil rig during the Christmas break. I can earn in excess of $3,000 if I work straight through and work overtime. I need the money, as I have to pay for my last semester at college and my apartment."

He gave her a gold necklace for Christmas. He asked her to consider moving in with him after New Year's. Brian said that today he would write his last exam. He had an opportunity to catch a ride to Winnipeg. His school friend was leaving after five p.m. Brian said that he would write her and to please think about his offer to live together. He kissed Mary Ann and then disappeared into the crowd of students moving past the cafeteria.

As she took the bus back to the residence, Mary Ann felt lonely. She realized that she could not count on Jamie anymore. She had not received a letter for three months. Brian was leaving again, and again she would have no one to share Christmas with. She remarked that there were only three people in the halfway house at Christmas. A new resident of Mexican background named Marie, who was on day parole from the prison, invited Mary Ann to attend midnight mass with her at the large Catholic cathedral. Mary Ann indicated that she had not gone to church since she was a young girl. She told me that she enjoyed the service and found peace inside the church walls. There were many university students at the service, since it was close to the university. Mary Ann joined Marie and attended church the following Sunday.

Mary Ann received her marks at the end of December, and this time she had a B-plus average. Her grades were improving each semester. She thanked Vivian for helping her last year to understand how to study and prepare for exams.

A letter arrived from Brian with a money order of $200 to buy some clothes and new shoes that she desperately required. He mentioned in his letter he would return to Kingston on January 8.

Mary Ann and Marie spent the days shopping and walking around the city. One day they were downtown and met an inmate who was out on unescorted temporary absence from the prison. Mary Ann inquired about Jamie. The inmate told her that Jamie was back in segregation for being drunk. Jamie had been removed from the wing with her black girlfriend. Again, Mary Ann never let on that she had gone out with Jamie.

For Mary Ann, 1987 began with the firm determination that she was going to complete her studies and obtain a full parole. She was undecided about moving in with Brian. The time went fast. On Monday, Mary Ann would start her last semester, hoping to graduate in May or June.

Changes to Female Prisons

Over the years, I met a number of very attractive inmates. A close friend of mine once asked me how I functioned inside with so many pretty ladies. I told him that it was true that some of the inmates were very attractive and sexy. I said that several inmates over the years flirted with me and wanted more, but I was not interested. I commented to my friend that I had developed a strong defence to help me cope with this reality. A wise colleague once suggested to me that the best defence is to consider all the inmates as sisters. I used that approach, and it helped me time and time again.

As the years went by, I observed some changes in the makeup of the correctional officers that were employed at the Prison for Women, which was opened in 1934. It was Canada's only federal prison for female offenders. At first, when female staff came to work at the prison, they would spend their entire career at the institution. There were no females working as correctional officers in male prisons. The majority of the female guards, or matrons as they were called in the early years, were primarily younger mothers with high school education or less. They were motherly and respectful to inmates and treated them fairly. Many of the inmates who entered the walls of the Prison for Women had serious emotional and mental health problems. The staff had to manage the inmate regardless of her sentence and the difficulties she posed to them. Because matrons worked closely with inmates and knew their problems, they were able to contain incidents from erupting and to prevent major disturbances or riots from occurring. Essentially, matrons talked to inmates and, by and large, gained their trust. It was like the jailer and the inmate were married to each other.

I reviewed the documents and found that the very first inmate had spent her entire adult life as a prisoner in the Prison for Women. In 1934, there was a young Ukrainian woman who was convicted of murder in Alberta and sentenced to hang. This inmate's sentence was commuted in December of 1934. She was sent to the Prison for Women. This inmate had a serious mental health problem that the staff could not help her with. She was admitted to the Kingston Psychiatric Hospital on March 16, 1935. She received a full parole to a rest home for mentally ill patients of the Kingston Psychiatric Hospital on May 24, 1978. She died on February 26, 1981, during the time I was warden. I never met this woman, but she was the longest-serving inmate on the books of the Prison for Women. Her inmate number was 01.

Isabel McNeill House (IMH)

The IMH is a century-old limestone building in Kingston, Ontario, located across the street from the former Prison for Women and kitty-corner to the maximum-security Kingston Penitentiary.

IMH operated for a number of years in the seventies as a halfway house (ten beds) for female offenders on conditional release to the community, prior to their final release. IMH closed in the latter part of the seventies, when it reopened in 1990 as a community correctional centre (minimum-security institution for female inmates).

The facility was appropriately named after Isabel McNeill, the first on-site Superintendent of the Prison for Women. Prior to her tenure as superintendent in the 1960s, the Prison for Women was a satellite of Kingston Penitentiary and managed by the male warden of the penitentiary.

The Correctional Service of Canada decided to close IMH in February 2007. They argued that the facility was too costly to operate because of its age and the high cost of maintenance.

IMH was Canada's only stand-alone Community Correctional Centre and minimum-security prison for women. A number of resident inmates of IMH appealed the closure to a Superior Court judge and the Court of Appeal for Ontario. They claimed that their constitutional rights would be violated if they were transferred to multi-level regional prisons, where they would be confined behind razor wire fences and under the watchful eye of security cameras. Their arguments were rejected. The inmates then applied to the Supreme Court of Canada, but failed to obtain a hearing (December 2008). The refusal of the Supreme Court to hear their case ended a two-year legal battle.

There are thirteen stand-alone, minimum-security prisons for men in Canada that do not have fences or armed guards.

Isabel McNeill House.
(Author)

I am confident that enlightened prison administrators in the future will eventually see the light and reconsider the merits of having a modern minimum-security facility for female offenders in an appropriate location in Canada. The current policy of having minimum-security inmates reside in a multi-level institution is a retrograde step and will eventually proved ill planned.

The last inmates at Isabel McNeill House were transferred to female multi-level institutions in December 2008.

Female Guards

As previously stated, the close relationship between correctional officers and correctional supervisors with the inmate population helped keep the lid on the prison. During the early eighties, our service started to employ female correctional officers in male institutions. It was a difficult beginning, since many male guards felt that there was no role for females as workers in male prisons. Some guards in certain prisons were so outraged that they tried to sabotage the process. They mistreated the few female guards and tried to get them to resign. Fortunately, the early female pioneers were able to withstand the negative introduction they received from some male guards.

By late 1987, I observed that the young guards who were entering the service were well educated, many of them with junior college degrees (Law and Security) and some with university degrees in the social sciences. The main problem I observed was that the female new recruits were not interested in working in the Prison for Women, but instead wanted to be employed in the male prisons. As the older female matrons were retiring, younger, well-educated women replaced them. Before I left my position as warden in late 1987, I observed that half of the female guards had less than three years in the service and all had been recent graduates of the staff college training program. The problem here was that the new recruits listed as their first and second choices to work in the male prisons. It seemed that few, if any, new female guards wanted to work at the Prison for Women.

We now had educated female guards who made their daily decisions strictly by the book. They did not want to be at the prison and they found it difficult to relate to the female offender. I thought that the situation would only get worse and create a climate of mistrust. Guards against inmates. A potential power keg was being created.

I remember a time, over thirty years ago, when other female personnel entered the prison and provided security duties and watched over female inmates.

In 1975, there was a national withdrawal of services of correctional officers that adversely affected all federal prisons in Canada, including the Prison for Women. On July 2, the guards walked off the job at twelve midnight, as mandated by their union. Management staff, including myself, correctional supervisors, and one male and one female staff member who were not correctional officers, were available to help run the prison.

Given the serious dilemma that federal institutions were facing across the country, the Government of Canada called in the army to provide physical security to each institution.

At the Prison for Women, we had twenty male and female armed soldiers positioning themselves at various points around the outer perimeter wall. I was totally convinced that the army could provide excellent security. No one would enter the prison and no inmate would escape.

At eight a.m., as I vividly recall, about twenty-four young female RCMP officers from the Ottawa area arrived at the prison. The majority of these police officers were recent graduates of the first and second class ever of female recruits entering the service in 1975. I was assigned four police officers to help supervise the inmates that were housed in Isabel McNeill House, the minimum-security halfway house located across the street from the prison. Two police officers worked twelve-hour shifts. I worked twenty-four hours straight the first day. All the female police officers were tall, lean, and in good shape. They were all intelligent and had excellent communication skills. They presented themselves very professionally.

Inside the main prison, the police officers manned the posts located outside all living units. They manned the front control post, and some officers were assigned to supervise the kitchen and the gymnasium area.

The other management representatives and I were so impressed with all the police officers that we wished we could have hired the entire group, had they been available. The RCMP had selected the best recruits and trained them very well; I suspected that the RCMP as an organization would utilize the various talents of the female officers in assigning them their various jobs and areas of responsibilities. Although the walkout lasted only less than two days, we encountered no problems from the inmates relating to the RCMP officers. The inmates were treated fairly and respectfully by the police officers.

In my view, the service missed the boat. It had had an opportunity to help correct the situation. I firmly believe that a separate training course should have been created and offered at the staff college for females and males who wanted to work at a female prison. I don't mean one- or two-week extra courses and lectures on the female prison, but a totally separate course with all graduates to be employed in a female facility. If you develop an environment where the correctional officers do not want to be, you are creating a potential milieu where adversaries compete for control of the prison.

West wall, the only wall structure still standing, March 2008.
(Author)

Mary Ann's Return to the Prison for Women

Mary Ann started her last semester in January 1987. During the end of the first week of the semester, she met Brian for lunch. He asked her if she wanted to live with him. She responded, "I will try a few weekends at your apartment. If we get along okay, I will consider moving in." Mary Ann got permission to spend Friday and Saturday night at Brian's house. Her parole officer was very helpful and suggested to Mary Ann that she take things slowly. During the next three weekends, Mary Ann spent time with Brian. The last Saturday night they had sex and were enjoying a smoke in bed and watching television. Brian continued to put more and more pressure on her to move in. Suddenly Mary Ann stood up and got dressed. She needed a beer. Mary Ann told Brian that she was an inmate like him and was residing at the halfway house. She said that she hoped to get a full parole in May. Brian wanted more sex and was demanding. Mary Ann saw something in Brian that concerned her. The more he drank the more aggressive and uglier he became.

Mary Ann was doing excellent work with her studies. She was now the second-place student with the highest marks. She was getting A's and B's in all her classes. Mary Ann told her parole officer about Brian's request to move in. She told Mary Ann she could not move in until she received full parole, and that most likely she would then be deported back to the United States.

Mary Ann spent the following weekend with Brian at his apartment. On Saturday, Brian left the apartment for twenty minutes to get more wine. During his absence, Mary Ann looked for a magazine and found several letters from Alberta. Mary Ann concluded that Brian was married and had a small child. About two minutes before Brian got back, the telephone rang. It was a long-distance call from a lady named Jo Ann. She asked where Brian was, and Mary Ann said that he would be back shortly.

Brian came back and they two drank two bottles of wine. Brian opened up and said that he was married with a small child but had been separated for six months. Mary Ann didn't tell Brian that a telephone call had come in from his wife. Brian got upset that Mary Ann would not move in with him. Mary Ann stated she could not move in because she was a lifer on day parole. Brian got very angry and wanted sex right away. Mary Ann started to cry and said that she could not go on this way. Her memory bank went back to San Francisco and her marriage to Willy and his request to have sex with two of his friends. Mary Ann got very upset and wanted to leave. At first Brian prevented her from leaving, but later he changed his mind. Mary Ann walked home, as she needed lots of fresh air.

The next four weeks were a difficult time for Mary Ann. Brian kept telephoning the halfway house asking for her. The other residents soon realized that Mary Ann had a tiger by the tail. Mary Ann decided to eat her lunch in the classroom and avoided the cafeteria. A friend of Mary Ann's told her that every lunch hour for the following four weeks, Brian was seen walking throughout the cafeteria looking for her.

Mouse felt betrayed by Brian. He had lied about being married; and later about when he had separated from his wife. He had said that he had no children; and later that he had a small child. The only thing Brian had told the truth about was the fact that he had been released from Frontenac Institution and that he was on full parole. Mary Ann weighed things carefully and realized that Brian would play no part of her future life.

Brian telephoned each day, sometimes two or three times. One day, Mary Ann met a friend of Brian's at a coffee shop located downtown. He was open with her and told her that Brian was married and that his relationship with his wife was not good. He further stated that Brian had been in jail before for drug possession and operating a stolen motor vehicle under the influence of drugs and alcohol. He also had a history of assaulting his wife.

One Sunday morning, Brian appeared at the halfway house. He asked to see Mary Ann. He was told that she was gone for the day. Mary Ann had left early with Marie and had gone to church and afterward planned to have a good breakfast. The house mother smelt alcohol and suggested that Brian call Mary Ann before coming to the house.

It was the first week of April, and Mary Ann could not get a good night's sleep. Her nerves were on edge. She made an appointment to see the psychiatrist. She entered the prison in the morning and saw the psychiatrist. He prescribed some medication for depression and anxiety. Mary Ann mentioned to me that she told the doctor she was having flashbacks about her failed marriage and trouble with her ex-husband. Furthermore, she indicated that she was having trouble sleeping and eating.

The next Saturday night, Brian came to the halfway house in an intoxicated state. He made some threats and scared the house supervisor. Mary Ann was afraid to be near this man.

On Monday, Mary Ann went to school and as she was entering her classroom Brian was waiting for her. He cried and stated that he loved her and wanted her to live with him. Mary Ann told Brian that she was not well and wanted nothing to do with him.

At the end of the week, Mary Ann completed her coursework, and all that was left was writing her final exams. Mary Ann was approached by Brian before she got on the bus to go home. He said that he needed to be with her and could not live anymore. Mary Ann was concerned for Brian's mental health and her safety. Later that afternoon, Mary Ann called her parole officer and said that she could no longer remain at the halfway house and wanted to return to the prison.

The parole officer got hold of me that day, as I was working late in my office on a special report. The parole officer was concerned for Mary Ann's safety and said she was not sleeping and eating normally. Within fifteen minutes, Mary Ann called and said she wanted to come back to the prison. I listened to her story and made arrangements with the Chief of Health Care and AW Security for Mary Ann to remain in the Health Care Centre until we could determine what was best for her.

On Monday morning, Mary Ann's parole officer entered the prison and met with her classification officer. After the meeting, the decision was made for Mary Ann to stay in the prison and reside in a vacant room in the wing and remain there until she received her full parole.

Mary Ann wrote all her exams within the next two weeks. She found the exams easy and was happy that the courses were over. Mary Ann did not socialize with other inmates in the wing as she waited for her exam marks. Within three weeks, she had received her marks and had a B-plus average. She got the highest mark in drafting and commercial designs.

Mary Ann found out that Jamie had been placed in segregation for sixty days after she assaulted another correctional officer in the segregation unit. She also learned that Jamie was not physically well, since she was infected with hepatitis C after sharing a needle with another inmate.

Within one week, Mary Ann asked to see me. I welcomed her as she entered my office. I spoke first: "Hi, Mouse. It's good to see you. I'm sorry that it did not work out well for you at the halfway house."

She looked me straight in the eye and said that she had served close to seven years and was ready to go back to New Mexico and see her mother. She hoped to get her children back after she had a job and her own apartment.

We talked for forty minutes. Mary Ann was mature now and realized that it was important that she not get involved further with Brian. She told me her story relating to Brian and her need to return to the prison. Mary Ann indicated that she wished Jamie well, but had no intention of contacting her.

Mary Ann received a letter that her parole hearing was scheduled for June 20, 1987. She received an unescorted temporary absence to attend her graduation. I went to the college and was very proud as I sat in the rear of the gymnasium watching as Mary Ann received her degree. She looked so happy. I congratulated Mary Ann and took her for coffee before returning to the prison. Mary Ann had accomplished a great deal since I first met her in 1980. She was mature, educated, and focused on her future. It was so rewarding to see an inmate progress and improve her life. She was not the young girl I met in Oakalla Provincial Jail. She was confident, well spoken, and enjoyed classical music. She was ready for the next stage of her life.

As warden I encountered many inmates in prison. It was so exhilarating when an inmate improved her life before your eyes. Equally it was depressing when a promising inmate turned to drugs, alcohol, or activities that did not conform to societal norms. In some cases, inmates did not improve after being incarcerated. All the programs and positive activities could not reach some inmates. They had been scarred badly as children and had received insufficient guidance and love during their formative years, resulting in their being unable to deal with life's experiences, whether they be up or down.

As for myself, I hated to leave the Prison for Women. I enjoyed my job and received very good evaluations. Something happened in the late eighties that changed how female prisons in Canada were run. Essentially, the chief administrators and bureaucrats of the Correctional Service of Canada were influenced by women's advocacy groups, female equality and legal advocates, and left-wing politicians. Decisions were made to appoint females to manage female prisons—not because they were more qualified, but because of their gender. The reality is that prisons should be governed by people not because of their sex but because they have had experience with, and an understanding of, the needs of female offenders.

I must admit that when I started at the Prison for Women I was green and, given the leadership and mentoring of my predecessor, I learned by craft. It was ironic, but in future years to come, females would most likely serve as wardens in male institutions across the land, and female institutions would essentially be managed by female wardens.

I was transferred briefly to Regional Headquarters and then assigned as District Director (Parole) for Eastern Ontario for approximately six months. Following the parole assignment, I was appointed warden of a male prison.

Mary Ann's Final Release

On June 20, 1987, Mary Ann was granted full parole. A three-member National Parole Board panel approved her full parole for deportation in twenty minutes. There were no inmates waiting outside when Mary Ann received her green light. I congratulated Mouse when she left the institution the next morning with only a small bag and a few books. She was transferred to the Elizabeth Fry halfway house for one week in order to complete some paperwork at the college, re-pack her belongings that were still at the halfway house, and purchase some new clothing. The Inmate

Sentence Administrator completed arrangements for Mary Ann to fly to New Mexico via Denver, Colorado, on June 28, 1987.

Mary Ann was going home shortly. She admitted that her offence had been pure madness. She was truly remorseful. She acknowledged that Jamie was very instrumental in her returning to the population and advancing her education. She stated that her involvement with Brian was a mistake. She further acknowledged that she had received excellent support from her teacher at the Prison for Women and her classification officer, as well as her parole officer from the Elizabeth Fry Society.

On the day Mary Ann was flying home, she telephoned me at the prison from the airport. She began by thanking me for my continued support for all her endeavours. She said that my support was instrumental in her obtaining success in her life.

Mary Ann opened up to me and shared some personal information. "Warden, I must be honest with you. When I first came to the Prison for Women, I was hot for you. You turned my crank. I hope you were not too upset with me sharing my intimate sexual encounter details with Jamie and Brian. In my strange way, I thought that if I shared my intimate thoughts with you, you would get turned on and be embarrassed."

I responded, "I've seen this page before. No, your intimate details were like water off a duck's back. Trust me when I tell you that other inmates were more open and deliberate in sharing their intimate thoughts and actions. It is part of the territory. I wasn't embarrassed."

Mary Ann continued, "I am glad that I got that off my chest. By the way, I changed my tattoo this past week. My mouse now has two large blue eyes." She hung up the phone after saying "Thank you."

Mary Ann returned home to New Mexico and visited her mother. I received a Christmas card from Mary Ann ten days before Christmas of the same year. She told me that she had moved to Southern California and was gainfully employed by a large architecture and engineering firm. She was earning a good salary, and she loved her work. She indicated that she had met a

Christian professional man at church and was very much in love. She had accepted his marriage proposal and within weeks would be married. She further stated that going to church with Marie while at the halfway house had brought her inner peace. Mary Ann wrote that she was converting to the Roman Catholic religion. She completed her little note by stating that she had contacted a very good law firm and was taking legal steps to obtain custody of her children. Her close friend from San Francisco told her where her children were residing. Finally, Mary Ann closed by saying that she had removed the string from her mouse's neck. I never heard from her again.

The Prison for Women closed on July 6, 2000.

The wall coming down.
(Courtesy Steven Wild, photographer)

REFERENCES

1. *Canadian Intermediate Dictionary* (Toronto: Gage Publishing Limited, 1979).

2. Simma Holt, *Terror in the Name of God* (Toronto: McClelland and Stewart Limited, 1964).

3. R.V.K. (1971) 3 CCC (2d) p. 84, Lacourciere, Judge (orally) (Ont. H.C.).

4. Frank Anderson, *Up the Latter* (Saskatoon: The Gopher Press, 1979).

5. *Commissioner's Directive 768*, Mother/Child Program, Correctional Service of Canada, 2003.

6. *The Vancouver Sun*, "RCMP Eyes Stalked Gang for Two Months" (June 9, 1984).

7. Supreme Court of Canada 1989, Judgment on Appeal for Ontario, Dec. 8, 1988.

DEFINITIONS

Executive Clemency—A decision by the Governor in Council under Royal Prerogative of Mercy (Cabinet of the Government of Canada) to release an offender from prison or to commute a sentence or to order the remission of all or part of a sentence.

LSD (Lysergic Acid Diethylamide)—A drug that can produce hallucinations and schizophrenic symptoms.

Mandatory Supervision (MS)—In 1969, the government enacted a bill that stated an inmate with accumulated remission of over sixty days was eligible for release. The inmate had to be released to serve his or her remitted time under supervision in the community, subject to the same conditions as any parolee.

Mules—Persons who transport illegal drugs into Canada.

Native Sisterhood—An Aboriginal inmate self-help group to help incarcerated female Native inmates.

Private Family Visiting (PFV)—Eligible inmates are allowed periodically to spend up to three days in a small house (private family visiting unit) with their husband, children, or family members; or by themselves. The unit was fenced off from the main prison yard. The inmate orders her food in advance and prepares the meals. The unit has a television and VCR for movie entertainment. The unit has an outside recreation area for children.

Remission Service—The agency that predated the Parole Board of Canada and instituted the beginning of parole in Canada.

Seg or Segregation—A special, secure area inside the prison that is isolated or separated from the main prison population. There are two sections inside the segregation area:

1. **Protective Custody (PC)**—Generally a small area that houses inmates who have requested protection from aggressive inmates because of the nature of their offence, debts, police informer, threats against their life, or because staff have received

information that they are at risk of physical harm.

2. **Dissociation or Punitive Segregation**—This area of segregation houses inmates that are involuntarily placed there by the warden because of disruptive or violent behaviour that adversely affects the good order of the institution; there is a risk of escape; they are awaiting disciplinary charges in disciplinary court; they have been sentenced in disciplinary court; they are in isolation because of medical reasons; or they are awaiting transfer to another secure facility.

Temporary Absence (TA), Escorted—After a period of time, eligible inmates are for a short duration allowed out of the institution, at first under escort, for socialization reasons: to visit a school, college, potential work placement, family, or a specialized counsellor; for shopping or a sporting event or for humanitarian reasons; or to visit a halfway house. A medical TA into the community is granted as required for medical reasons.

Temporary Absence (TA), Unescorted—After a period of time, eligible inmates are allowed to leave the prison for up to three days to visit with family in their own community. Depending on the offence and length of the sentence, the TA is approved by the warden or the National Parole Board.

Ticket of Leave—Beginning of parole. On August 11, 1899, an Act to provide for the conditional liberation of convicts—The Ticket of Leave—was enacted by the Canadian Parliament and was a form of pardon.

ABBREVIATIONS AND ACRONYMS

AA — Alcoholics Anonymous

CSC — Correctional Service of Canada

ICP — Independent Chairperson

IERT — Institutional Emergency Response Team

INTERPOL — International Criminal Police Commission

IPSO — Institutional Preventive Security Officer

PFW; P4W — Prison for Women

RCMP — Royal Canadian Mounted Police

ABOUT THE AUTHOR

George Caron was born and raised in Vancouver's lower mainland. He is the oldest of seven children. He is proud of his Metis background. He graduated from Western Washington State University in 1967 with a degree in psychology, anthropology, and sociology. He received his Master of Social Work degree (MSW) in 1971 from the University of Calgary.

He worked in a variety of social welfare and children's services before commencing a career in adult corrections. He had a career of thirty-five years with the Correctional Service of Canada. He was first employed as a federal parole officer in Alberta. During the seventies and eighties, up to the end of 1987, he was assistant warden and then warden of the Prison for Women. After leaving the P4W, he was assigned as District Director of Parole for Eastern Ontario for approximately six months and was then appointed warden of a male prison. Before retiring in 2007, he was involved in national investigations with the CSC.

George's unique personal experiences in working with male and female parolees and inmates have broadened his horizons. It has helped him gain immeasurable insight into, and understanding of, the many complex issues facing troubled human beings.

George lives in Ontario with his wife and two children, two dogs, one chicken, and one goose.

MOUSE ON A STRING
AT THE
PRISON FOR WOMEN

GEORGE CARON

TO ORDER MORE COPIES, CONTACT:

General Store Publishing House
499 O'Brien Road, Box 415
Renfrew, Ontario, Canada K7V 4A6
Tel 1-800-465-6072 • Fax 1-613-432-7184

www.gsph.com